Births, Marriages and Deaths on the Web

SECOND EDITION

PART 2
The Midlands, Northern England and East Anglia

Stuart A. Raymond

FEDERATION OF FAMILY HISTORY SOCIETIES (PUBLICATIONS) LIMITED

Published by
The Federation of Family History Societies (Publications) Ltd
Units 15-16, Chesham Industrial Centre
Oram Street, Bury,
Lancashire BL9 6EN

in association with
S.A. & M.J. Raymond
P.O.Box 35, Exeter, EX1 3YZ

First Published 2002
Second edition, 2005

FFHS (Publications) Ltd: ISBN: 1 86006 190 7
S.A. & M.J. Raymond ISBN: 1-899668-42-X

Printed and bound at the Alden Press, Osney Mead, Oxford OX2 0EF

Contents

Introduction

The records of births, marriages and deaths are vital resources for family historians. A rapidly increasing number of transcripts and indexes of these records are now available on the internet, and it is the purpose of this directory to identify the many web-pages where they can be found. Pages rather than sites are listed, as one site can include pages for numerous different places – Genuki being the obvious example.

This directory is primarily concerned with civil registration and parish records, although associated records such as bishops transcripts, marriage licences, *etc.* are also mentioned. I have not, except in a few cases, listed the pages of particular registry offices, nor have I included pages devoted solely to particular surnames. Monumental inscriptions and war memorials are the subjects of separate directories.

The titles of each page are given as they appear on the page; if no title is given on the page I have indicated this by enclosing my own wording in square brackets. If the title does not indicate the period covered I have tried to indicate this in a note. If the page is an index, rather than a transcript, this is also noted (although not entirely consistently). Where the page is taken from a book, a brief bibliographic note is included. Incidentally, a transcript is not an index, nor an index a transcript. A transcript is an attempt to copy a document exactly as it is written; an index is an alphabetical list of the terms (in our case, names) in that document, indicating where they can be found. These are quite distinct terms, although they are often confused in the pages listed below. Be suspicious of web pages where such confusion is found (I have tried to indicate them). A web master who is inaccurate in this is quite likely to be inaccurate elsewhere too.

It is noticeable that, although a few facsimiles of published registers have been mounted on the web, there are no facsimiles of the original documents. It is therefore, necessary to repeat the exhortation with which all good genealogical authors encourage their readers: check your sources! A transcript or index is only as accurate as the transcriber or indexer. Some are very good indeed; others are awful! If at all possible, you should always go back to the original record and check it.

This directory is equally liable to human error. If you are unable to find a URL listed here, you should enter either a part of the URL itself, or words from the title, into a search engine such as **www.google.com**. URL's change frequently, and no doubt a small proportion of those listed here will be out of date within a few months of publication. If you are still unable to find a site, it may have been removed from the web. Even so, it may still be possible to consult it. A vast number of old web pages are archived at **www.waybackmachine.org.** If you are unable to find any web page mentioned in this book, you should search its URL on this site. The Wayback Machine can also be used to locate a number of sites identified in the first edition of this book which have since been removed from the internet; a number of these are indicated below.

If you come across errors in this book, URL's that have changed, or new pages that ought to be listed, please let me know. It is hoped to produce new editions at frequent intervals, in order to help you keep track of the information currently available on the web.

This book has been typed by Cynthia Hanson, and seen through the press by Bob Boyd. My thanks go to them, and also to the officers of the Federation of Family History Society, whose support is vital to my work. My wife Marjorie, is also to be thanked for insisting that I should turn the computer off occasionally!

Stuart A. Raymond

General

Civil Registration

- General Register Office: Births, Deaths and Marriages Registration
  www.gro.gov.uk/gro/content/
- Family Records Centre
  www.familyrecords.gov.uk/frc/
- A Comedy of Errors Continued ... The Marriage Records of England and Wales
  globalgazette.net/gazfd/gazfd.38.htm
- Barbara's Registration Web Page: Certificate Information
  home.clara.net/dixons/Certificate/indexbd.htm
  General information on obtaining certificates
- Ordering Birth Registration Certificates from England and Wales using the LDS Family History Center's Resources
  www.oz.net/~markhow/ukbirths.htm
- UK Certificates.com
  www.ukcertificates.com/
  Commercial service

Civil Registration Indexes

- Free BMD
  freebmd.rootsweb.com
  Project to index civil registration records,; includes gateway to a number of indexes to district registrars registers
- General Register Office Indexes 1837-1997
  www.westsussex.gov.uk/content/libraries-and-archives/record-office/family-history/general-register-office-indexes.jsp?g11n.enc=UTF-8
  Indexes for the whole country available at the West Sussex Record Office
- General Register Office Indexes
  www.hants.gov.uk/record-office/gro.html
  Prepared by the Hampshire Record Office, but of country-wide interest.
- General Register Office Indexes
  www.shropshireonline.gov.uk/archives.nsf
  Click on 'What we hold', and title.
- A Guide to Civil Registration in Great Britain
  www.gmcro.co.uk/family_history/st_caths.htm
  On the site of Greater Manchester County Record Office
- England and Wales Civil Registration Index 1837-1900
  www.ancestry.co.uk/search/rectype/vital/freebmd/main.htm
- The St. Catherine's Marriage Index
  www.cs.ncl.ac.uk/genuki/StCathsTranscriptions
  Introduction to a collection of transcriptions, some of which are listed under appropriate counties in this directory
- Birth, Marriage and Death Certificates
  www.familyhistoryonline.co.uk/database/UnrelatedCerts.shtml/
  Index of certificates donated to the Birmingham & Midland Society of Genealogy & Heraldry

Proposed Changes to Civil Registration

- Select Committee on Regulatory Reform: Second Report
  www.publications.parliament.uk/pa/cm200405/cmselect/cmdereg/118/11803.htm
  House of Commons report on proposed civil registration reforms
- Delegated Powers and Regulatory Reform: Third Report
  www.publications.parliament.uk/pa/ld200405/ldselect/lddelreg/14/1402.htm
  House of Lords report on the proposals
- Civil Registration: Vital Change: Birth Marriage and Death Registration in the 21st Century
  www.official-documents.co.uk/document.cm53/5355/5355.pdf
  Government proposals for the future of the service
- Government White Paper: Civil Registration: Vital Changes
  www.ffhs.org.uk/Societies/Liaison/WhitePaper.htm
  The F.F.H.S. response to the White Paper
- Civil Registration: Delivering Vital Change: Response from the Society of Genealogists
  www.sog.org.uk/files/crr2003finalresponse.html

Parish & Non-Parochial Registers: Introductory Pages

- Parish Registers
  www.jaydax.co.uk/genlinks/registers.html
  General discussion, especially of northern registers

- Parish Registers (and nonconformist records), England and Wales
  www.familyrecords.gov.uk/topics/religious.htm

- English Parish Registers
  www.british-genealogy.com/resources/registers/indexf.htm
  Introductory guide

- Catholic Central Library Mission Registers
  www.catholic-library.org.uk/registers.html
  List of register transcripts available

- The Library, Friend's House, London: Genealogical Sources
  www.quaker.org.uk/library/geneal.htm
  Includes information on the important Quaker 'digests' of births, marriages and deaths.

- Births, Marriages and Deaths at Sea
  www.catalogue.nationalarchives.gov.uk/RdLeaflet.asp?sLeafletID=246

- Births, Marriages and Deaths Overseas
  www.history.ac.uk/gh/overseas/
  Leaflet from Guildhall Library, London

Indexes

- Family Search
  www.familysearch.org
  Click on 'search' for the *International genealogical index*

- British Isles Vital Records Index, 2nd ed. Breakdown of Records
  www.genoot.com/downloads/BVR12/
  Lists registers covered

- IGI Batch Numbers: British Isles and North America
  freepages.genealogy.rootsweb.com/~hughwallis/IGIBatchNumbers.htm

- The LDS Family Search C Website: Using the Batch Numbers
  globalgazette.net/gazfd/gazfd36.htm

- Batches Extracted from Dr. William's Non-Conformist Registers
  freepages.genealogy.rootsweb.com/~hughwallis/IGISpecialBatches.htm#DrWilliams

- Boyd's Marriage Index 1538-1840
  www.britishorigins.com/help/popup-aboutbo-bmi2.htm
  Subscription database

- Births, Marriages, and Deaths at Sea 1854-1890
  www.nationalarchivist.com/index03/about.cfm
  Pay per view database

- FreeREG
  freereg.rootsweb.com/
  Project to provide free internet searches of parish registers

- The Institute of Heraldic and Genealogical Studies: Library Search Facilities
  www.ihgs.ac.uk/library/search_facilities.php
  Lists a variety of indexes to registers, *etc.* held by the Institute

- Marriage Database
  www.uk-genealogy.org.uk/datafiles/marriagesearch.html
  Index to selected marriage registers from Cornwall, Leicestershire, Lincolnshire, Rutland & Somerset; almost 4,000 entries.

- United Kingdom Marriages, 1838-1972
  www.jewishgen.org/databases/UK/marriages.html
  Jewish marriages from civil and synagogue registers

- National Burial Index for England and Wales
  www.ffhs.org.uk/General/Projects/NBI.htm
  Details of a major project to index burials on CD

- Jewish Gen Online Worldwide Burial Register
  www.jewishgen.org/databases/Cemetery/
  Over25,000 UK entries

- Parish and Probate Records
  www.allvitalrecords.com/ukisearch.asp
  Database of 15,000,000+ records from England, Wales, Scotland and Ireland

- Ted Wildy's Marriage Witness Index
  www.genuki.org.uk/mwi/

- Marriage Witness Indexes
  members.optushome.com.au/guthrigg/mwi.htm

Marriage Licences

- Marriage Licence Allegations Index 1694-1850: Vicar-General and Faculty Office
  www.britishorigins.com/help/popup-aboutbo-mla2.htm
  Subscription database

Transcripts on the Web

- English Parish Records
  www.obliquity.com/family/parish/
  Collection of excerpts from parish registers for selected surnames, covering Norfolk, Northamptonshire, Somerset, Suffolk, & Westmorland. The individual pages are not listed separately here.

- Genogold: Local Records
  www.genogold.com/html/local_records.html
  Collection of searchable databases for eight different counties

- Parish Registers
  www.parishregisters.co.uk
  freepages.genealogy.rootsweb.com/~pinks
  Collection of transcripts from various counties

- UK Transcriptions Web-Site
  uk-transcriptions.accessgenealogy.com
  Collection of parish register transcripts, *etc.,* separately listed below

- United Kingdom Genealogy: Parish Registers
  www.uk-genealogy.org.uk/Registers/index.html
  Collection of parish registers available on the web, and listed separately elsewhere in this directory. Some also available on CD

Publications

- English Parish Records
  shops.ancestry.com/subcat.asp?shopid=126&CatID=520
  Parish registers on CD from Ancestry.com

- Archive CD Books: Church & Cemetery Registers
  www.rod-neep.co.uk/books/types/registers/
  General discussion of registers and transcripts which are being published on CD

- England and Wales Genealogy & History on CD ROM
  globalgenealogy.com/countries/england/cdrom.html
  Includes many registers on CD

- British Isles CD-Roms
  www.quintinpublications.com/cdengland.html
  Includes many parish registers on CD

- National Index of Parish Registers
  www.samjraymond/btinternet.co.uk/natipareg.html
  Details of the authoritative published guide to the whereabouts of original registers and transcripts

- TWR Computing
  www.twr computing.freeserve.co.uk
  Many parish registers on CD for sale

Miscellaneous

- Common Latin Words
  www.genealogy.doun.org/transcriptions/help/latin_words.php
  Commonly found in parish registers

- Prohibited Marriages
  www.badsey.net/history/prohib.htm
  List from the *Book of Common Prayer,* 1662

Bedfordshire

Civil Registration

- Registration District in Bedfordshire
  www.fhsc.org.uk/genuki/REG/bdf.htm
  Between 1837 and 1930

- [St. Catherine's House Marriage Index, Jan-March, 1849. District 6. Bedfordshire/Berkshire/Hertfordshire]
  www.cs.ncl.ac.uk/genuki/StCathsTranscriptions/CATH4906.TXT

Parish and Non-Parochial Registers: Introductions and Lists

- About Bedfordshire Records
  www.rootsweb.com/~engbdf/records.html
  Mainly concerned with parish registers and associated records

- Anglican Parish Registers
  www.bedfordshire.gov.uk/BedsCC/sdcountyrec.nsf/
  Enter and click on title. Lists registers at Bedfordshire and Luton Records Office. Almost all pre-1813 registers have been published

- Non-Anglican Registers
  www.bedfordshire.gov.uk/BedsCC/sdcountyrec.nsf/
  Enter and click on title. Lists registers at Bedfordshire and Luton Archives and Records Office

- Non-Ecclesiastical Birth and Death Registers
  www.bedfordshire.gov.uk/BedsCC/sdcountyrec.nsf/
  Enter and click on title

- Bedfordshire Parish Registers in Bedfordshire Libraries
  www.galaxy.bedfordshire.gov.uk/webingres/bedfordshire/vlib/0.local_studies/parish_registers.htm
  List of printed transcripts and fiche of original registers in local libraries

- Bedfordshire
  www.sog.org.uk/prc/bedford.html
  Parish registers, printed, typescript, *etc.,* in the library of the Society of Genealogists

- Bedfordshire: Quaker Family History Society
  www.rootsweb.com/engqfhs/Research/counties/beds.htm
  Lists registers *etc.*

Indexes

- Bedfordshire Parish Registers: Preparing a Master Index
  www.sigg.org.uk/arts/arts2601.htm
  Article from the Society of Indexers Genealogical Group

- Bedfordshire, England: Parish and Probate Records
  www.beliefnet.ancestry.com/search/rectype/inddbs/5843.htm
  www.ancestry.com/search/db.aspx?dbid=5843
  Database based on published registers, *etc.*

- IGI Batch Numbers for Bedford, England
  freepages.genealogy.rootsweb.com/~hughwallis/IGIBatchNumbers/CountyBedford.htm

- Parishes covered by Boyd's Marriage Index: Bedfordshire
  www.britishorigins.com/help/popup-aboutbo-bmi-countydetails.htm
  Click on 'Bedfordshire'

- Free Reg: Bedfordshire
  freereg.rootsweb.com/parishes/bdf/index.htm
  Details of the registers currently included in a project to index births, deaths and marriages

- National Burial Index (Bedfordshire FHS)
  www.familyhistoryonline.co.uk/database/NBIBedfordshireFHS.shtml
  Pay per view

Publications

- Bedfordshire Parish Register Series
  www.kbnet.co.uk/brianp/publications.html#two
  Bedfordshire is unique in having all its pre-1812 registers available in printed form or on fiche. The fiche are listed here.

Great Barford

- Great Barford Parish Records
  www.sgibbs1.freeserve.co.uk/gtbarford/
  Indexes to baptisms 1831-1892; marriages 1813-1904; burials 1841-1904.

Kempston

- Parish Register of Kempston (1570-1812)
  www.yourtotalevent.com/places/Bedfordshire/Kempston.html
  General discussion, with list of registers

Lidlington

- Lidlington, Bedfordshire
  www.genogold.com/html/bedfordshire1.html
  Database of early registers

Toddington

- Toddington Family History Resource Page
  www.toddington.net/hist.htm
  Baptisms, 1540-61; marriages, 1558-99, 1653-1739 & 1800-1812, and burials, 1558-1600; banns 1754-1812

Turvey

- Turvey's Non-conformists
  www.turvey.homestead.com/nonconform.html
  Includes list of burials in the graveyard of Turvey Reformed Church

Cambridgeshire

Civil Registration

- Registration Districts in Cambridgeshire
  www.fhsc.org.uk/genuki/REG/cam.htm

- Cambridgeshire District Registrars
  www.genealogy-links.co.uk/html/cam.dist.reg.html

- Births, Marriages and Deaths: Cambridgeshire Index Project
  www.cambridgeshire.gov.uk/sub/register/cambsindex.htm
  Project to index Cambridgeshire civil registers

- [St. Catherine's House Marriage Index. Jan-March, 1849. District 14. Cambridgeshire/Lincolnshire]
  www.cs.ncl.ac.uk/genuki/StCathsTranscriptions/CATH4914.TXT

Parish & Non-Parochial Registers: Introduction & Lists

- Original Parish Registers at the County Record Office, Cambridge
  www.genuki.org.uk/big/eng/CAM/OriginalParishRegisters.html
  List

- Microfilm Holdings of Parish Registers & Bishops Transcripts at the County Record Office, Cambridge
  www.genuki.org.uk/big/eng/CAM/CambridgeshireRecordOfficeMicrofilmHoldings.html
  List

- Wisbech & Fenland Museum
  www.geocities.com/tmbsgen/museum.html
  Includes list of Cambridgeshire and Norfolk parish registers held

- Cambridgeshire
  www.sog.org.uk/prc/cambridgeshire.html
  Parish registers, printed, typescript, etc., in the library of the Society of Genealogists

- Cambridgeshire Methodism
  www.rootsweb.com/~engcam/method.htm
  Lists Methodist registers

- Quaker Family History Society: Cambridgeshire
  www.rootsweb.com/~engqfhs/Research/counties/cambs.htm
  Lists Quaker registers, *etc.*

- Cambridgeshire Society of Friends (Quakers)
  www.rootsweb.com/~engcam/quakers.htm
  Includes notes on registers

Indexes

- Cambridgeshire Baptism Index 1801-37
  www.cfhs.org.uk/BaptismIndex/
  On-line database

- Cambridgeshire Family History Society: Boyds Marriage Index 1538-1600
  www.cfhs.org.uk/BoydsMarriageIndex/index.html
  Searchable database for Cambridgeshire

- Cambridgeshire Burial Index (1801-1837)
  www.cfhs.org.uk/BurialIndex/
  On-line database

- Parishes covered by Boyds Marriage Index: Cambridgeshire
  www.britishorigins.com/help/popup-aboutbo-bmi-countydetails.htm
  Click on 'Cambridgeshire'

- Cambridgeshire, England: Parish and Probate Records
  www.ancestry.co.uk/search/db.aspx?dbid=5851
  Index to published registers, *etc.*

- IGI Batch Numbers for Cambridge, England
  freepages.genealogy.rootsweb.com/~hughwallis/IGIBatchNumbers/CountyCambridge.htm
  For Cambridgeshire

- National Burial Index (Cambridgeshire F.H.S.)
  www.familyhistoryonline.co.uk/database/NBICambsFHS.shtml

- Search Dr. Williams Library Index
  www.cfhs.org.uk/DrWilliams/index.html
  Index to 1200 Cambridgeshire nonconformist births, 1742-1837

Transcripts on the Web

- Cambridgeshire Family History Society Parish Register Transcript Microfiche Available
  www.cfhs.org.uk/parregmf.html

Strays

- Cambridgeshire Family History Society Strays: Marriages and banns
  www.rootsweb.com/~engcam/Strays/StraysMarriagesBanns.html

Cambridge

- Search Cambridge St. Clements Parish Register Index
  www.cfhs.org.uk/CambridgeStClements/index.html
  Searchable database to registers available on fiche

Chatteris

- Chatteris Burial Records
  jonspage.users.btopenworld.com/BurialRegisters/BurialRegIndex.html
  Index

- Parish Records Site
  jonspage.users.btopenworld.com/Parish/parish.html
  Submitted entries from Chatteris registers

Christchurch

- Christchurch Parish Registers: Transcript Index
  freepages.genealogy.rootsweb.com/~cawthorn/TRANSCRIPTS/
  Brief extracts, 19-20th c.

Ely

- Cholera in the 19th century
  www.rootsweb.com/~engcam/cholera.htm
  Includes list of Ely victims 1832

Fenstanton

- Fenstanton Genealogical Searches
  www.ti0/fenstanton/historical/genealogical__search.htm
  Details of offline indexes

Leverington

- Leverington Marriage Index 1626-1675
  www.cfhs.org.uk/LeveringtonMarriages1626-1675/
  Database

Orwell

- The Marriage Register of the Parish of Orwell 1653 to 1837
  www.orwell.uk.com/orwell%20marriage%20register.htm

Thorney

- Thorney Baptisms: index of selected baptisms found in the parish register (Church of England) for Thorney Cambridgeshire, from 1653-1800
  contueor.com/wisbech/indexes/thorney.htm

Wimpole

- Parish Registers, St. Andrew's Parish Church, Wimpole
  www.wimpole.uk.com/wimpole_registers.htm
  Baptisms 1560-99; banns 1754-1863; marriages 1700-1863; burials 1560-1863

Wisbech

- Wisbech and the Fenlands: Indexes
  contueor.com/wisbech/indexes/index.htm
  Collection of indexes to parish registers of the district, including a combined index. The district includes mainly Norfolk parishes, although Wisbech itself is in Cambrideshire.

- Wisbech St. Mary Marriages: index of selected marriages found in the Parish Register for Wisbech St. Mary, Cambridgeshire from 1744-1803
  contueor.com/wisbech/indexes/wisbech_m.htm

- Wisbech St. Peter Baptisms: Index of Selected Baptisms found in the parish register for Wisbech St. Peter, Cambridgeshire, from 1559-1830
  contueor.com/wisbech/indexes/wis_p_bp.htm
- Index of Selected Marriages from 1560-1827, for Wisbech St. Peter, CAM., England
  contueor.com/wisbech/indexes/wis_p.htm

Cheshire

Civil Registration

- Registration Districts in Cheshire
  www.fhsc.org.uk/genuki/REGg/chs.htm
  Between 1837 and 1930

- Cheshire Registration Service
  www.cheshire.gov.uk/register/home.htm

- Cheshire BMD: Births, Marriages and Deaths on the Internet
  cheshirebmd.org.uk
  Index in progress, covering civil registration records 1837-1950. Important

- [St. Catherine's House Marriage Index, Jan-March, 1849. District 19. Cheshire/Derbyshire]
  www.cs.ncl.ac.uk/genuki/StCathsTranscriptions/CATH4919.TXT

- [St. Catherine's House Marriage Index, Jan-March, 1849. District 18. Cheshire/Shropshire]
  www.cs.ncl.ac.uk/genuki/StCathsTranscriptions/CATH4918.TXT

Parish and Non-Parochial Registers: Introductions & Lists

- Cheshire
  www.sog.org.uk/prc/cheshire.html
  Parish registers, printed, typescript, *etc.,* in the library of the Society of Genealogists

- Quaker Family History Society: Cheshire
  www.rootsweb.com/engqfhs/Research/counties/cheshire.htm
  Notes on Quaker records

Indexes

- Parishes covered by Boyds Marriage Index: Cheshire
  www.britishorigins.com/help/popup-aboutbo-bmi-countydetails.htm
  Click on 'Cheshire'

- North Cheshire Family History Society: Cheshire Burial Database
  www.genuki.org.uk/big/eng/CHS/NorthChesFHS/NBIPrintService.htm
  Details of an off-line index

- National Burial Index (North Cheshire F.H.S.)
  www.familyhistoryonline.co.uk/database/NBINCheshireFHS.shtml
  Pay per view

- Burials of Non-Residents in North and East Cheshire
  www.familyhistoryonline.co.uk/database/CHSBurialsNonResident.shtml
  Pay per view

- IGI Batch Numbers for Cheshire, England
  freepages.genealogy.rootsweb.com/~hughwallis/IGIBatchNumbers/CountyCheshire.htm

- Cheshire Parish and Probate Records
  www.ancestry.com/search/db.aspx?dbid=5856
  Index to published registers

Marriage Licences *etc.*

- Marriage (Licences & Bonds) 1639-1765
  www.geocities.com/fountalnpen/marriages2.html
  For Cheshire, mainly at Witton, Northwich, Great Budworth *etc.*

- Chester Marriage Licence Bonds February - [April] 1825
  homepages.rootsweb.com/~mwi/che1825f.txt
  Continued as follows:
  1825 May-August **/che1825m.txt**
  1825 December **/che1825d.txt**
  1826 January **/che1826j.txt**

Transcript Collections on the Web

- Cheshire Parish Register Project
  www.csc.liv.ac.uk/~cprdb
  Project to transcribe all Cheshire registers. Those already available and fully described (as at April 2002) are separately listed below. Many other parishes are well-advanced. Currently, only access by form-filling is available to casual users. Important

Publications

- Family History Society of Cheshire. Publications
  www.fhsc.org.uk/fhsc/pubs.htm
  Many parish registers available on fiche; also marriage indexes on CD

- North Cheshire Family History Society: Cheshire Parish & Non-Conformist Register Transcripts
  www.genuki.org.uk/big/eng/CHS/NorthChesFHS/Cheshire_Burials.htm

- Family History Society of Cheshire: Crewe Group
  www.scfhs.org.uk/scfhs/pubs.html
  List of publications, including parish registers

Bromborough

- Parish Notes: Bromborough 1600-1870
  www.csc.liv.ac.uk/~cprdb/Notes/Parish/BROB.html
  Discussion of entries in Cheshire Parish Register Project (see above)

Burton

- Parish Notes: Burton 1538-1870
  www.csc.liv.ac.uk/~cprdb/Notes/Parish/BROB.html
  Discussion of entries in Cheshire Parish Register Project (see above)

Chester

- Methodist Death Notices from St. John Circuit, Chester, 1803-1900
  www.geocities.com/Heartland/Plains/8555/obit.html
  This page has been removed from the web, but has been archived at **www.waybackmachine.org**

Cuddington

- A few Cuddington Marriages 1692-1719
  www.geocities.com/brigaban/cuddmarr.html

Disley

- St. Mary's Church Registers
  www.disley.net/disley_pr.html
  At Disley, Cheshire. Marriages from Phillimore's published transcript, 1591-1738/9; selected baptism and burial entries

Heswall

- Parish Notes: Heswall 1539-1871
  www.csc.liv.ac.uk/~cprdb/Notes/Parish/HESW.html
  Discussion of entries in Cheshire Parish Register Project (see above)

Kelsall

- Parish Registers, Kelsall, Cheshire
  www.the-dicksons.org/Kelsall/kelsall/parish.htm
  Includes St. Philips marriage register 1869-99, and extracts from Kelsall Methodist church burial register 1916-88.

Little Budworth

- Burials, Little Budworth Parish Register 1921-1938
  www.geocities.com/brigaban/burialslitbud.html

Middlewich

- Middlewich Cemetery
  www.pctecnics.co.uk/html/middlewich_cem.html
  Burials from 1867

Nantwich

- A Complete List of Soldiers buried at Nantwich during the years of the Great Civil War, as recorded in the parish register
  www.geocities.com/brigaban/solciv.html

Neston

- Parish Notes: Neston 1559-1871
  www.csc.liv.ac.uk/~cprdb/Notes/Parish/NEST.html
  Discussion of entries in the Cheshire Parish Register Project

Overleigh

- Overleigh Cemetery Database Online
  www.cheshire.gov.uk/recoff/LACOverleighCemetery/home.asp
  Index to the registers, 1850-91, with 19,000 entries

Taxall

- St. James's of Taxall Church Records
  www.disley.net/taxal_pr.html
  Baptisms 1610-1904; marriages 1611-1867; burials 1610-1875

Weaverham

- Weaverham Marriages (at least one partner from Weaverham parish, or marriage took place at Weaverham)
  www.geocities.com/brigaban/weavmarr.html
  From Chester Cathedral register

West Kirby

- Parish Notes: West Kirby 1561-1871
  www.csc.liv.ac.uk/~cprdb/Notes/Parish/WKIR.html
  Discussion of entries in Cheshire Parish Register Project (see above)

Whitegate

- Parish Notes: Whitegate 1565-1971
  www.csc.liv.ac.uk/~cprdb/Notes/Parish/WHTG.html

Woodchurch

- Parish Notes: Woodchurch 1571-1871
  www.csc.liv.ac.uk/~cprdb/Notes/Parish/WODC.html
  Discussion of entries in the Cheshire Parish Register Project (see above)

Cumberland

Civil Registration

- Registration Districts in Cumberland
  www.fhsc.org.uk/genuki/REG/cul.htm
  Between 1837 and 1930

- Cumbria Genealogy: the St. Catherine's Marriage Index for March quarter, 1849
  janelittle.members.beeb.net/Miscellaneous/StCatsMarchQr1849Marriages.html
  For Cumberland and Westmorland

Parish and Non-Parochial Registers: Introductory and Lists

- Cumberland
  www.sog.org.uk/prc/cumberland.html
  Parish registers, printed, typescript, *etc.,* in the library of the Society of Genealogists

- Parishes in Cumberland which are listed at the Cumberland Record Office, Carlisle, as having years missing from the I.G.I.
  members.madasafish.com/~cgrs/igi.htm

- Quaker Family History Society: Cumberland
  www.rootsweb.com/~engqfhs/Research/counties/cumberlnd.htm
  Notes on Quaker records (including the Isle of Man)

Indexes

- Cumbrian Genealogy: Parish Registers Index
  www.btinternet.com/~grigg/ParRegsIndex.htm

- Parishes covered by Boyds Marriage Index: Cumberland
  www.britishorigins.com/help/popup-aboutbo-bmi-countydetails.htm
  Click on 'Cumberland'

- IGI Batch Numbers for Cumberland, England
  freepages.genealogy.rootsweb.com/~hughwallis/IGIBatchNumbers/CountyCumberland.htm

Transcript Collections on the Web

- The Cumberland Family History Site
  www.cumberlandroots.co.uk
  Includes parish register indexes

- Some Bishops' Transcripts of Cumberland, England
  www.reayw.freeserve.co.uk/
  Collection of transcripts

- Cumbrian Genealogy: Parish Registers
  johnwatters.members.beeb.net.htm
  Many pages of transcripts for Cumberland and Westmorland, separately listed below. These pages have been removed from the web, but are archived at **www.waybackmachine.org**

Publications

See also Durham

- C.W.A.A.S. Publications
  www.cwaas.org.uk/publications.html
  Includes a few parish registers

Allhallows

- Bishops' Transcripts of Allhallows Parish, Cumberland 1663-1837
  www.reayw.freeserve.co.uk/alltran.htm
  Transcript and index

Allonby

- Chapelry of Allonby: Baptisms and Burials 1774-1837
  members.madasafish.com/~cgrs/Allonby.htm
  Index

Alston

- Cumbrian Genealogy: Alston Marriages 1701-1783
  johnwatters.members.beeb.net/AlstonAtoG.htm
  Index continued on 3 further pages. These pages have been removed from the web, but are archived at **www.waybackmachine.org**

- Marriages from the Alston registers (1701-1783)
  www.genuki.org.uk/big/eng/CUL/Alston/MALS1701.html
  Continued as follows:
  1784-1812 **/MALS1784.html**
  1813-1837 **/MALS1813.html**

Aspatria

- Aspatria St. Kentigerns Parish Church Baptism Register 9 January 1813 to 20 June 1847
  members.madasafish.com/~cgrs/Aspatria.htm
  Transcript and index

Bassenthwaite

- The Oldest Parish Registers of Bassenthwaite
  janelittle.members.beeb.net/Miscellaneous/Bassenthwaite.html
  Originally published in the *Transactions of the Cumberland & Westmorland Antiquarian & Archaeological Society* 1965 for selected names only. Extracts

Beckfoot

- Quaker Marriages recorded at Beckfoot 1772-1910
  members.madasafish.com/~cgrs/BeckfootMarriages.htm

Bromfield

- Bromfield Parish Registers: Baptisms & Marriages 1813-1837; Burials 1654-1916; Bromfield Churchyard Monumental Inscriptions
  members.madasafish.com/~cgrs/Bromfield.htm

Dearham

- Dearham Bishops' Transcript 1663-1837
  www.reayw.freeserve.co.uk/deaidx.htm
  Transcript and index

Flimby

- Flimby Bishops' Transcripts 1713-1812
  www.reayw.freeserve.co.uk/flitran.htm
  Transcript and index

Garrigill

- Baptisms from the Garrigill registers 1813-1837
  www.genuki.org.uk/big/eng/CUL/Garrigill/XGAR.html
- Marriages from the Garrigill Registers 1730-1837
  www.genuki.org.uk/big/eng/CUL/Garrigill/MGAR.html

Gilcrux

- Gilcrux Bishops Transcripts 1663-1837
  www.reayw.freeserve.co.uk/giltran.htm
  Transcript and index

Great Orton

- The Registers of the Parish Church of St. Giles, Great Orton, Cumberland
  content.ancestry.com/iexec/?htx=BookList&dbid=28930&ti=O8r=0
  Pay per view
- Cumbrian Genealogy: Parish Register of St. Giles, Gt. Orton 1568-1812
  johnwatters.members.beeb.net/~rolygrigg/OrtonABC855.htm
  Index, continued on 4 further pages. These pages have been removed from the web, but are archived at
  www.waybackmachine.org

Holme Cultram

- Holme Cultram Section
  www.madasafish.com/barrylawman/page5.html
  Includes bishops' transcripts 1663-1871, & indexes of marriages 1871-1914, & burials 1871-1902

Holme St. Cuthbert

- Holme St. Cuthbert Baptisms, Marriages and Burials 1850-1900
  www.madasafish.com/~cgrs/HSTCBAPS.htm
  Indexes

Holme St. Paul

- [Holme St. Paul]
  myweb.tiscali.co.uk/barrylawman/page9.html
  Indexes to baptisms, marriages, and burials, 1850-1900

Lamplugh

- Cumbrian Genealogy Lamplugh Parish Register 1581-1812
  johnwatters.members.beeb.net/LamplughAB910.htm
  Index continued on 6 further pages. These pages have been removed from the web, but are archived at
  www.waybackmachine.org

Matterdale

- Matterdale and Watermillock
  edenlinks.rootsweb.com/1gp/RECORDS/MATTEX.HTM
  Includes Matterdale register 1634-57, marriages 1634-1910, Wesleyan Methodist Chapel of Matterdale and Watermillock baptisms register, *etc.*

Newton Reigny

- Cumbrian Genealogy: Newton Reigny Parish Register 1571-1812
  johnwatters.members.beeb.net/NewtonReignyAtoG.htm
  Continued on 3 further pages. Thes pages have been removed from the web, but are archived at **www.waybackmachine.org**

Penrith

- Cumbrian Genealogy: The Registers of St. Andrew's Parish Church, Penrith
  johnwatters.members.beeb.net/Penrith1AtoB.html
  Index continued on 6 further pages, 1556-1604. These pages have been removed from the web, but are archived at **www.waybackmachine.org**

- Cumbrian Genealogy: The Registers of St. Andrew's Parish Church, Penrith
  johnwatters.members.beeb.net/Penrith2AtoB.html
  Index continued on 7 further pages, 1605-1660. These pages have been removed from the web, but are archived at **www.waybackmachine.org**

Silloth

- Index to Marriages at Silloth, Christ Church, 1871 to 1910
  members.madasafish.com/~cgrs/SILMAR.htm

Skelton

- Cumbrian Genealogy: Skelton Parish Register 1680-1812
  johnwatters.members.beeb.net/SkeltonAB.htm
  Continued on 9 further pages. These pages have been removed from the web, but are archived at **www.waybackmachine.org**

Stapleton

- Stapleton Parish Church
  members.madasafish.com/~cgrs/STAPBAP.htm
  Indexes to baptisms, marriages, and burials, 1813-1839

Watermillock

See Matterdale

Westnewton

- Westnewton St. Matthews Parish Church
  members.madasafish.com/~cgrs/Westnewton.htm
  Index to marriages, 1662-1978

Wigton

- Wigton Parish
  myweb.tiscali.co.uk/barrylawman/page4.html
  Includes bishops' transcripts 1604-1797, marriages 1781-1797, burials 1813-1855; Catholic Chapel marriages 1832-55, and cemetery records index, 1855-84.

- Wigton Bishops' Transcripts 1798-1812
  www.reayw.freeserve.co.uk/wigidx.htm
  Transcript and index

- Cumbrian Genealogy: The Parish Registers of Wigton, Cumberland: Baptisms 1604-1727
  johnwatters.members.beeb.net/wig1bap1.html
  Continued on 2 further pages. These pages have been removed from the web, but are archived at **www.waybackmachine.org**

- Cumbrian Genealogy: Registers of Wigton: Baptisms 1729-1797
  johnwatters.members.beeb.net/wig2bap1.html
  Index continued on 3 further pages.. These pages have been removed from the web, but are archived at **www.waybackmachine.org**

- Cumbrian Genealogy: The Parish Registers of Wigton Cumberland: Marriages 1604-1727
  johnwatters.members.beeb.net/wig1mar1.html
  Index continued on 2 further pages. These pages have been removed from the web, but are archived at **www.waybackmachine.org**

- Cumbrian Genealogy: Registers of Wigton: Marriages 1728-81
  johnwatters.members.beeb.net/wig2Marr1.html
  Index continued on 3 further pages. These pages have been removed from the web, but are archived at **www.waybackmachine.org**

- Cumbrian Genealogy: The Registers of Wigton: Burials 1604-1727
  johnwatters.members.beeb.net/wig1bur1.html
  Continued on 3 further pages. These pages have been removed from the web, but are archived at **www.waybackmachine.org**

- Cumbrian Genealogy: Registers of Wigton: Burials 1728-1779
  johnwatters.members.beeb.net/wig2bur1.html
  Continued on 2 further pages. These pages have been removed from the web, but are archived at **www.waybackmachine.org**

Derbyshire

Civil Registration

- Registration Districts in Derbyshire
  www.fhsc.org.uk/genuki/REG/dby.htm
  Between 1837 and 1930

- Derbyshire District Registrars
  www.genealogy-links.co.uk/html/dby.dist.reg.html
  Addresses

- Derbyshire Registrars Marriage Index
  www.familyhistoryonline.co.uk/database/DBYRegMarrIndex.shtml
  Pay per view

Parish & Non-Conformist Registers: Introductory Pages & Lists

- Derbyshire Record Office and Derby Diocesan Record Office: A Brief History of the Registers of the Church of England
  www.derbyshire.gov.uk
  Click on 'catalogues and indexes' and title. Includes list of registers held

- Derbyshire Ancestral Research Group Church of England Registers
  www.genuki.org.uk/big/eng/DBY/DARG/CERegisters.html
  List of transcripts held

- The Derbyshire Ancestral Research Group Nonconformist Registers
  www.genuki.org.uk/big/eng/DBY/DARG/NCregisters.html
  List of transcripts held

- Derbyshire
  www.sog.org.uk/prc/derbyshire.html
  Parish registers, printed, typescript, etc., in the library of the Society of Genealogists

- Quaker Family History Society: Derbyshire
  www.rootsweb.com/~engqfhs/Research/counties/derby.htm
  Notes on Quaker records

Indexes

- Free Reg: Derbyshire
  freereg.rootsweb.com/parishes/dby/index.htm

- Parishes covered by Boyd's Marriage Index: Derbyshire
  www.britishorigins.com/help/popup-aboutbo-bmi-countydetails.htm
  Click on 'Derbyshire'

- National Burial Index (Derbyshire Ancestral Research Group)
  www.familyhistoryonline.co.uk/database/NBIDARG.shtml
  Pay per view

- Derbyshire, England: Parish and Probate Records
  www.ancestry.com/search/db.aspx?dbid=5863.htm
  Index of published registers

- Free Reg: Derbyshire
  freereg.rootsweb.com/parishes/dby/index.htm
  Details of the registers currently included in a project to index births, marriages and deaths.

- IGI Batch Numbers for Derby, England
  freepages.genealogy.rootsweb.com/~hughwallis/IGIBatchNumbers/CountyDerby__(A-M).htm
  Continued at **/CountyDerby__(N-Z).htm**

Publications

- Publications
  www.merton.dircon.co.uk/drspubs.htm
  List of Derbyshire Record Society publications, including a few parish registers

Transcript Collections on the Web

- UK Genealogy Archives: Derbyshire
  www.uk-genealogy.org.uk/england/Derbyshire/
  Includes collection of pages from Phillimore's published transcripts of registers

- Derbyshire: Records of Marriages in individual parishes
  homepages.ntlworld.com/sherwoodoutlaw/derbyshiremarriageindex.htm
  Pages for individual parishes separately listed below

- North West Derbyshire Sources
  freepages.genealogy.rootsweb.com/~dusk/
  Collection of transcripts and indexes

- Repton & Gresley Hundred, South Derbyshire: Parish Register Transcripts
  freepages.genealogy.rootsweb.com/~brett/parregs.htm

Allestree

- Marriages at Allestree 1595 to 1812
  www.uk-genealogy.org.uk/england/Derbyshire/towns/a/Allestree/index.html
  Facsimile of the published Phillimore transcription

Alvaston

- Marriages at Alvaston 1614 to 1812
  www.uk-genealogy.org.uk/england/Derbyshire/towns/a/Alvaston/index.html
  Facsimile of the published Phillimore transcription

- Alvaston 1614-1812: Brides
  homepage.ntlworld.com/sherwoodoutlaw/alvastonbride.htm
  Index. For an index of grooms, see **/alvastongroom.htm**

Ashbourne

- Matters of life and death: history in baptisms, marriages and burials as recorded in the parish registers of St. Oswald's Parish Church, Ashbourne, Derbyshire, England, 1539 to 1945
  www.ashbourne-town.com/history/life.htm
  Selected extracts only

Ashover

- Baptisms, Marriages and Burials at All Saints Church, Ashover
  www.genuki.org.uk/big/eng/DBY/Ashover/CDAllSaints.html
  Details of a CD

- Ashover: a guide for genealogists
  www.ashover.com
  dspace.dial.pipex.com/goth/
  Includes baptisms, marriages and burials, 17-20th c., also Methodist and Quaker registers

- Weddings at All Saints Church, from 1642-1724
  familytreemaker.genealogy.com/users/m/i/l/John-Mills/FILE/0003page.html
  At Ashover

Bakewell

- Baptisms, Marriages and Burials at All Saints, Bakewell
  www.genuki.org.uk/big/eng/DBY/Bakewell/CDAllSaints.html
  Details of a CD

Baslow

- Extracts of Baslow Parish Records
  www.genuki.org.uk/big/eng/DBY/Baslow/Records.html
  Index to parish registers and other records

- Some Notes from Baslow Parish Registers 1688-1737, 1738-51, 1752-1804
  www.genuki.org.uk/big/eng/DBY/Baslow/PRNotes.html
  Mainly notes; few baptisms, marriages and deaths.

Blackfordby

- Blackfordby St. Margaret Parish Page
  freepages.genealogy.rootsweb.com/~brett/blackfordby/blackfordby.html
  Includes bishops' transcripts 1630-1895, baptisms 1630-1895, marriages 1630-1701 & 1832-3, & burials 1630-1895 (with index).

Boulton

- Marriages at Boulton, 1756 to 1812
  www.uk-genealogy.org.uk/england/Derbyshire/towns/b/Boulton/index.html
  Facsimile of the published Phillimore transcription

Bradwell

- Bradwell Parish Registers
  freepages.genealogy.rootsweb.com/~dusk/bradwell_pr.html
  Selected burials 1869-78

- Bradwell Primitive Methodists Burials 1846-Feb.1864
  freepages.genealogy.rootsweb.com/~dusk/bradwell_prim_meth.html

Brailsford

- Derbyshire Parish Registers: Marriages at Brailsford 1653 to 1812
  www.uk-genealogy.org.uk/england/Derbyshire/towns/b/Brailsford/index.htm
  Facsimile of the published Phillimore transcription

Brampton

- Brampton (Derbyshire) Information about Brampton Church Records
  www.genuki.org.uk/big/eng/DBY/OldBrampton/ChurchRecords.html

- Baptisms, Marriages and Burials at St. Peter & Paul's Church, Old Brampton
  www.genuki.org.uk/big/eng/DBY/OldBrampton/CDStPeter.html
  Details of a CD

- Old Brampton Deaths & Burials
  www.genuki.org.uk/big/eng/OldBrampton/Burials.html
  Index of the parish register and monumental inscriptions, 19-20th c.

Brassington

- Brassington Residents Database
  www.brassington.org/database.htm
  Index to parish registers and various other sources

Breaston

- Marriages at Breaston 1719 to 1820
  www.uk-genealogy.org.uk/england/Derbyshire/towns/b/Breaston/index.html
  Facsimile of the published Phillimore transcription

Brimington

- Brimington
  www.skimber.demon.co.uk/brim/brim.htm
  Includes births/baptisms and burials/deaths from various sources, 20th c.

Castleton

- Castleton Parish Registers
  freepages.genealogy.rootsweb.com/~dusk/Castleton_pr.html
  Selected burials, 1784-1820

Cauldwell

- Cauldwell Online Resources: Databases
  freepages.genealogy.rootsweb.com/~blanchec/cauldindex.htm
  Includes bishops' transcript baptisms 1666-1869, marriages 1666-1929, & burials 1666-1869
- Melbourne General Baptist Baptisms: Cauldwell Residents 1774-1784
  freepages.genealogy.rootsweb.com/~blanchec/caldgenbaps.htm

Chaddesden

- Chaddesden 1718 to 1812
  www.uk-genealogy.org.uk/england/Derbyshire/towns/c/Chaddesden/index.html
  Facsimile of the published Phillimore transcription

Chapel en le Frith

- St. Thomas a Beckett Parish Registers
  freepages.genealogy.rootsweb.com/~dusk/chapel-e-l-f_pr.htm
  Baptisms (selected) 1621-1874; marriages (selected) 1622-1862, and burials (selected) 1622-1907.
- BUNTING, WM. BRAYLESFORD *The parish church of St. Thomas a Becket, Chapel-en-le-frith 1225-1925.* 1925
  www.marchington.pwp.blueyonder.co.uk/02/
  Facsimile of a printed book. Scroll down and click on '8: The Parish Registers'
- Chapel: Wesleyan Methodist Chapel Burials 1882-1904. Selected entries only
  freepages.genealogy.rootsweb.com/~dusk/chapel_wes_chapel.html

Charlesworth

- St. Mary's Independent Chapel, Charlesworth
  freepages.genealogy.rootsweb.com/charlesworth_in_chapel.htm
  Selected baptisms 1786-1833, and burials 1852-1904

Chellaston

- Marriages at Chellaston 1570 to 1812
  www.uk-genealogy.org.uk/england/Derbyshire/towns/c/Chellaston/index.html
  Facsimile of the published Phillimore transcription
- Chellaston 1570-1812: Grooms
  homepage.ntlworld.com/sherwoodoutlaw/chellastongroom.htm
  Index. For an index of brides, see **/chellastonbride.htm**

Chesterfield

- Chesterfield, Derbyshire: B.V.R.I.
  www.connorsgenealogy.com/Derbyshire/Chesterfield/bvri.htm
  List of Chesterfield names in the *British vital records index* CD.
- The Dissenters Register
  homepages.rootsweb.com/~spire/chesterfield/dissenters.htm
  Originally published in *The history of Chesterfield,* 1890. Covers 1710-32. This page appears to have been removed from the web, but is archived at **www.waybackmachine.org**

Chinley

- Chinley Independent Chapel
  freepages.genealogy.rootsweb.com/~dusk/chinley_ind_chapel.html
  Includes baptisms 1727-1840, marriages (selected), 1887-1918 and burials (incomplete) 1703-1908
- Chinley Wesleyan Chapel Baptisms 1809-1823. Selected Entries only
  freepages.genealogy.rootsweb.com/~dusk/chinley_wes_chapel.bapt.html

Church Broughton

- Marriages at Church Broughton 1538 to 1812
  www.uk-genealogy.org.uk/england/Derbyshire/towns/c/ChurchBroughton/index.html
  Facsimile of the published Phillimore transcription

Church Gresley

- Church Gresleys' St. Mary & St. George: Parish Page
  freepages.genealogy.rootsweb.com/~brett/gresley/gresley.htm
  Includes list of registers, transcripts, films, *etc;* also baptisms 1841-60, marriages 1783-1883, & burials 1695-1812 (transcripts & indexes).

Coton in the Elms

- Coton in the Elms Parish Page
  freepages.genealogy.rootsweb.com/~brett/coton/coton.html
  Includes transcripts & indexes of baptisms 1846-82, marriages 1868-1901 & burials 1846-1901

Crich

- Crich Parish Registers: Marriage, Baptism, Burial
  freepages.genealogy.rootsweb.com/~dlhdby/parish.htm
  Baptisms, marriages & burials, 1813-25

Dale Abbey

- Marriages at Dale Abbey 1667 to 1813
  www.uk-genealogy.org.uk/england/Derbyshire/towns/d/DaleAbbey/index.html
  Facsimile of the published Phillimore transcription

Darley Dale

- Baptisms, Marriages and Burials at St. Helen's Church, Darley Dale
  www.genuki.org.uk/big/eng/DBY/DarleyDale/CDStHelen.html
  Details of CD

Derby

- Derbyshire Parish Registers: Marriages at St. Alkmunds, Derby, 1539 to 1812
  www.uk-genealogy.org.uk/england/Derbyshire/towns/s/St.Alkmund/index.html
  Facsimile of the published Phillimore transcription
- St. Michael's, Derby, 1559 to 1812
  www.uk-genealogy.org.uk/england/Derbyshire/towns/d/DerbyStMichaels/index.html
  Facsimile of the published Phillimore transcription
- Derbyshire Parish Registers: Marriages at St. Peter's, Derby, 1558 to 1812
  www.uk-genealogy.org.uk/england/Derbyshire/towns/d/DerbyStPeter/index.html
  Facsimile of the published Phillimore transcription
- Derby St. Peter's 1558-1812: Grooms
  homepage.ntlworld.com/sherwoodoutlaw/derbystpetersfrontpage.htm.htm
  Index. For brides, see: **/derbystpetersbridefrontpage.htm**
- Brook Street, Derby: General Baptist Births
  freepages.genealogy.rootsweb.com/~blanchec/BrookBirths.htm
  Covers 1792-1806. Continued for 1815-30 at **/BrookBirths2.htm**

Dethick

- Parish Registers
  freepages.genealogy.rootsweb.com/~dlhdby/parishreg.htm
  Dethick baptisms 1774-1781 and 1813-1820.

Donisthorpe

- Oakthorpe & Donisthorpe
  freepages.genealogy.rootsweb.com/~brett/donisthorpe/donisthorpe.htm
  Includes list of parish registers, transcripts, films, *etc.* with index of Donnisthorpe burials, 1838-1848

Duffield

- Duffield 1598 to 1812
  www.uk-genealogy.org.uk/england/Derbyshire/towns/d/Duffield/index.html
  Facsimile of the published Phillimore transcription.
  Continued at **/Duffield2/Index.html**
- Parish Registers and Churchwardens Books
  www.derwent99.freeserve.co.uk/duffield/11rgstr.htm
  General discussion of the Duffield register. Not a transcript.

Eckington

- Eckington (Derbyshire) Some Births & Baptisms (1800-1892)
  www.genuki.org.uk/big/eng/DBY/Eckington/Baptisms.html
  Index of selected entries
- Eckington (Derbyshire) Some Deaths & Burials (1811-1894)
  www.genuki.org.uk/big/eng/DBY/Eckington/Burials.html
  Index of selected entries

Edale

- Edale Parish Registers
  freepages.genealogy.rootsweb.com/~dusk/edale_pr.html
  Selected burials, 1813-36

Elmton

- Baptisms, Marriages and Burials for Elmton, Derbyshire
  www.familyhistoryonline.co.uk/database/DBYElmton/shtml
  Pay per view

Elton

- Baptisms, Marriages and Burials at All Saints Church, Elton
  www.genuki.org.uk/big/eng/DBY/Elton/CDAllSaints.html

Eyam

- Extracts of Eyam Parish Records
  www.genuki.org.uk/big/eng/DBY/Eyam/Records.html
  Names from a variety of sources, including the parish register, bishops transcripts, monumental inscriptions, *etc.*

- The Plague Book of Eyam
  www.geocities.com/Heartland/Acres/8040/plague.html
  Includes list of plague victims 1666.

- *The history and antiquities of Eyam,* by William Wood. 1842, 1845 & 1860.
  www.genuki.org.uk/big/eng/DBY/Eyam/Wood/index.html
  Includes extracts from the burials register, 1665-6.

Foremark

- Foremark & Ingleby Parish Pages
  freepages.genealogy.rootsweb.com/~brett/foremark/foremark.html
  Includes baptisms from the bishops' transcripts 1662-1887, and burials 1813-1987 (with indexes)

- Marriages at Foremark, 1663 to 1837
  www.uk-genealogy.org.uk/england/Derbyshire/towns/F/Foremark/index.html
  Facsimile of the published Phillimore transcription

Glossop

- All Saints Church, Glossop: Selected Entries Only
  freepages.genealogy.rootsweb.com/~dusk/glossop_pr.html
  Baptisms 1620-1857; marriages 1632-1907; burials 1621-1859

- Whitfield Independent, Glossop p. Burials
  freepages.genealogy.rootsweb.com/~dusk/whitfield_ind.html
  Burials 1828-1838

Hartshorne

- Hartshorne.org.uk
  www.hartshorne.org.uk/Content/Archive/
  Click on 'Births', 'Marriages', 'Deaths', or 'Parish registers'. Under construction.

- Hartshorne Parish Page
  freepages.genealogy.rootsweb.com/~brett/hartshorne/hartshorne.html
  Includes baptisms 1594-1812, marriages 1594-1898, & burials 1594- 1902; also bishops' transcripts, 1701-1801

Hathersage

- Hathersage Parish Registers
  freepages.genealogy.rootsweb.com/~dusk/hathersage_pr.html
  Selected burials, 1813-18

Hault Hucknall

- Marriages at Hault Hucknall 1660 to 1812
  www.uk-genealogy.org.uk/england/Derbyshire/towns/h/HaultHucknall/index.html
  Facsimile of the published Phillimore transcription

Hayfield

- St. Matthew Church, Hayfield
  freepages.genealogy.rootsweb.com/~dusk/hayfield_pr.html
  Selected baptisms, 1747-1880, and burials, 1640 to 1918

- Hayfield Bethel Chapel
  freepages.genealogy.rootsweb.com/~dusk/bethel_chapel.html
  Baptisms 1842-1900; marriages 1909-16

Heage
See Heanor

Heanor

- Heanor and Heage Ancestral Archives Materials Page
  www.spendlovej.freeserve.co.uk/ancestral/archives.html
  Includes Heage baptisms 1819-38, marriages 1847-1897 & burials 1847-78; also Heanor baptisms 1816-94.

Heath

- Marriages at Heath, *alias* Lownd, or Lund, 1682 to 1812
  www.uk-genealogy.org.uk/england/Derbyshire/towns/h/Heath/index.html
  Facsimile of the published Phillimore transcription

Hope

- Hope Parish Registers
  freepages.genealogy.rootsweb.com/~dusk/hope_pr.html
  Baptisms 1601-38; marriages 1636-40; burials 1598/9-1816
- Notes from a Peakland Parish: an account of the Church and Parish of Hope in the County of Derby, chapter V: Some Notes on the Parish Register
  www.genuki.org.uk/big/eng/DBY/Hope/Notes/ChapterV.html
  General discussion with some extracts

Horsley

- Marriages at Horsley 1558 to 1812
  www.uk-genealogy.org.uk/england/Derbyshire/towns/h/Horsley/index.html
  Facsimile of the published Phillimore transcription

Ilkestone

- Derbyshire Parish Registers: Marriages at Ilkeston 1588 to 1812
  www.uk-genealogy.org.uk/england/Derbyshire/towns/i/Ilkeston/index.html
  Facsimile of the published Phillimore transcription

Ingleby
See Foremark

Kirk Hallam

- Kirk Hallam, 1700 to 1837
  www.uk-genealogy.org.uk/england/Derbyshire/towns/k/KirkHallam/index.html
  Facsimile of the published Phillimore transcription

Kirk Ireton

- Kirk Ireton 1572 to 1798
  www.uk-genealogy.org.uk/england/Derbyshire/towns/k/KirkIreton/index.html
  Facsimile of the published Phillimore transcription

Kirk Langley

- Marriages at Kirk Langley, 1654 to 1812
  www.uk-genealogy.org.uk/england/Derbyshire/towns/k/KirkLangley/index.html
  Facsimile of the published Phillimore transcription
- Kirk Langley 1654-1812: Grooms
  homepage.ntlworld.com/sherwoodoutlaw/kirklangleygroom.htm
  Index. For an index of brides, see **/Kirklangleybride.htm**

Lownd
See Heath

Mackworth

- Marriages at Mackworth 1603 to 1812
  www.uk-genealogy.org.uk/england/Derbyshire/towns/m/Mackworth/index.html
  Facsimile of the published Phillimore transcription

Marple Bridge

- Independent Chapel, Mill Brow, Marple Bridge
  freepages.genealogy.rootsweb.com/~dusk/mill_brow_ind.html
  Burials, 1835 & 1837

Matlock

- Marriages at Matlock, 1637 to 1812
  www.uk-genealogy.org.uk/england/Derbyshire/towns/m/Matlock/index.html
  Facsimile of the published Phillimore transcription

- Matlock Surnames from Baptism, Marriage and Burial entries found in the parish registers for Matlock, Derbyshire, England, 1637-1856
  www.wirksworth.org.uk/MK-X-01.htm

- Baptisms, Marriages and Burials at St. Giles Church, Matlock
  www.genuki.org.uk/big/eng/DBY/Matlock/CDStGiles.html
  Details of a CD

- Hatches, Matches and Dispatches
  www.andrewspages.dial.pipex.com/matlock/reg/
  Baptisms 1662-1856; marriages 1637-1837; burials 1662-1856. Also Glenorchy Chapel baptisms, 1705-1836, & U.R.C. deaths, 1867-80

Melbourne
See also Cauldwell

- Melbourne & Packington General Baptist Baptisms 1765-1770
  freepages.genealogy.rootsweb.com/~blanchec/MelbGBbap.htm
  Continued as follows:
  1771-5 **/MelbGBbap2.htm** 1776-80 **/MelbGBbap3.htm**
  1781-84 **/MelbGBbap4.htm** 1787-94 **/MelbGBbap5.htm**
  N.B. these are adult baptisms

- Melbourne General Baptist births 1753-1781
  freepages.genealogy.rootsweb.com/~blanchec/MelbBirths.htm

Mellor

- St. Thomas's Parish Church, Mellor
  freepages.genealogy.rootsweb.com/~dusk/mellor_pr.html
  Marriages, 1678-1775, from the published Phillimore transcript; also selected baptisms 1631-1914 and burials 1624-1918

- Marriages at Mellor 1678 to 1775
  www.uk-genealogy.org.uk/england/Derbyshire/towns/m/Mellor/index.html
  Facsimile of the published Phillimore transcription

Monyash

- Quaker Marriages - Monyash
  dspace.dial.pipex.com/goth/quakmar.htm
  1678-89

Morton

- Morton 1575 to 1812
  www.uk-genealogy.org.uk/england/Derbyshire/towns/m/Morton/index.html
  Facsimile of the published Phillimore transcription

Netherseal

- Netherseal & Overseal Parish Pages
  freepages.genealogy.rootsweb.com/~brett/seal/seal.htm
  Includes detailed list of registers, with transcripts & indexes of St. Peter's baptisms, marriages & burials, 1725-1812, and of St. Matthew's baptisms & burials, 1842-71

New Brampton

- New Brampton (Derbyshire): Information about New Brampton Church Records
  www.genuki.org.uk/big/eng/DBY/NewBrampton/ChurchRecords.html

- New Brampton (Derbyshire) Births & Baptisms
  www.genuki.org.uk/big/eng/DBY/NewBrampton/Baptisms.html
  Index 1832-1903

- New Brampton (Derbyshire) Deaths & Burials
  www.genuki.org.uk/big/eng/DBY/NewBrampton/Burials.html
  Index, 1832-1974

New Mills

- New Mills
  freepages.genealogy.rootsweb.com/~dusk/newmills.html
  Includes marriages 1837-1901, Quaker burials 1865-72, Independent burials 1832-7

Newbold

- Newbold (Derbyshire)Some Births & Baptisms (1857-1906)
  www.genuki.org.uk/DBY/Newbold/Baptisms.html
  Index

- Newbold (Derbyshire) Deaths & Burials
  www.genuki.org.uk/big/eng/DBY/Newbold/Burials.html
  Index, 1857-1927

Newhall

- Newhall Baptisms 1833
  freepages.genealogy.rootsweb.com/~brett/newbap33.htm
  Continued to 1882 on annual pages, with separate surname index
- Newhall Marriages 1845-1850
  freepages.genealogy.rootsweb.com/~brett/newmar50.htm
  Continued to 1877, with separate surname index on 8 further pages
- Newhall Burials 1833
  freepages.genealogy.rootsweb.com/~brett/newbur33.htm
  Continued to 1865 on annual pages, with separate surname index on 6 pages
- Parish Records: [Newhall]
  www.geocities.com/emmamassey82/bmd.html
  Selected entries only

Newton Solney

- Newton Solney Baptisms 1663-1675
  freepages.genealogy.rootsweb.com/~brett/nsbap1663__1675.htm
  Continued to 1761, with separate surname index on 8 further pages
- Newton Solney Marriages 1663-1754
  freepages.genealogy.rootsweb.com/~brett/nsmar1663-1754.htm
  Continued to 1836, with surname index on 5 further pages
- Newton Solney Burials 1663-1675
  freepages.genealogy.rootsweb.com/~brett/nsbur1663__1675.htm
  Continued to 1812, with surname index on 10 further pages

Normanton

- Normanton-by-Derby, 1769 to 1810
  www.uk-genealogy.org.uk/england/Derbyshire/towns/n/Normanton/index.html
  Facsimile of the published Phillimore transcription
- Normanton by Derby 1769-1810: Grooms
  homepage.ntlworld.com/sherwoodoutlaw/normantongroom.htm
  Index. For an index of brides, see **/normantonbride.htm**

North Wingfield

- Baptisms, Marriages and Burials at St. Lawrence's Church, North Wingfield
  www.genuki.org.uk/big/eng/DBY/Northwingfield/CDStLawrence.html
  Details of a CD, including some entries for Clay Cross and Pilsley

Norton

- Marriages at Norton, 1559 to 1812
  www.uk-genealogy.org.uk/england/Derbyshire/towns/n/Norton/index.html
  Facsimile of the published Phillimore transcription

Oakthorpe

See Donisthorpe

Ockbrook

- Marriages at Ockbrook 1631 to 1812
  www.uk-genealogy.org.uk/england/Derbyshire/towns/o/Ockbrook/index.html
  Facsimile of the published Phillimore transcription

Old Brampton

See Brampton

Osmaston

- Marriages at Osmaston-by-Derby, 1743 to 1812
  www.uk-genealogy.org.uk/england/Derbyshire/towns/o/Osmaston/index.html
  Facsimile of the published Phillimore transcription
- Osmaston by Derby 1743-1812: Grooms
  homepage.ntlworld.com/sherwoodoutlaw/osmastongroom.htm
  Index. For an index of brides, see **/osmastonbride.htm**

Overseal

See Netherseal

Peak Forest

- The Marriage Registers of Peak Forest Chapel, Derbyshire
  www.genuki.org.uk/big/eng/DBY/PeakForest/about.html
  From the edition edited by G. W. Marshall and published in 1901

- Peak Forest Parish Registers
  freepages.genealogy.rootsweb.com/~dusk/peak_forest_pr.html
  Selected burials only, 1813-21
- Foreign Marriages in Peak Forest Chapel 1727-1754
  www.genuki.org.uk/big/eng/DBY/PeakForest/pftext.html
- Other Marriages in Peak Forest Chapel 1729-March 1815
  www.genuki.org.uk/big/eng/DBY/PeakForest/pftext2.html

Peasonhurst
See Ashover

Pilsley
See North Wingfield

Pinxton
- Pinxton 1561-1812: Brides
  homepage.ntlworld.com/sherwoodoutlaw/pinxtonbrides.htm
  Index. For an index of grooms, see **/pinxtongrooms.htm**

Quarndon
- Marriages at Quarndon, 1755 to 1812
  www.uk-genealogy.org.uk/england/Derbyshire/towns/q/Quarndon/index.html
  Facsimile of the published Phillimore transcription

Risley
- Marriages at Risley, 1720 to 1812
  www.uk-genealogy.org.uk/england/Derbyshire/towns/r/Risley/index.html
  Facsimile of the published Phillimore transcription

Sandiacre
- Marriages at Sandiacre, 1581 to 1812
  www.uk-genealogy.org.uk/england/Derbyshire/towns/s/Sandiacre/index.html
  Facsimile of the published Phillimore transcription

Spondon
- Marriages at Spondon, 1653 to 1812
  www.uk-genealogy.org.uk/england/Derbyshire/towns/s/Spondon/index.html
  Facsimile of the published Phillimore transcription

Stanley
- The Stanley One Place Study
  freepages.genealogy.rootsweb.com/~alanbloor/SOPS.htm
  Includes searchable database of baptisms, marriages and burials; also of bishops' transcripts and some Wesleyan Methodist baptisms
- Marriages at Stanley 1754 to 1812
  www.uk-genealogy.org.uk/england/Derbyshire/towns/s/Stanley/index.html
  Facsimile of the published Phillimore transcription

Stanton by Dale
- Derbyshire Parish Registers: Marriages at Stanton-by-Dale 1605 to 1812
  www.uk-genealogy.org.uk/england/Derbyshire/towns/s/StantonbyDale/index.html
  Facsimile of the published Phillimore transcriptions

Stapenhill
- Stapenhill Online Resources
  freepages.genealogy.rootsweb.com/~blanchec/StapOPC.htm
  Includes baptisms 1770-1800, marriages 1771-1825 & burials 1813-1862
- Stapenhill Baptisms 1770-1779
  freepages.genealogy.rootsweb.com/~brett/stabap01.htm
  Continued to 1800, with surname index, on 5 further pages

Stoney Middleton
- Extracts of Stoney Middleton Parish Records
  www.genuki.org.uk/big/eng/DBY/StoneyMiddleton/Records.html
  Index of registers and other sources

Swadlincote
- Swadlincote Parish Pages
  freepages.genealogy.rootsweb.com/~brett/swadlincote/swadlincote.html
  Includes transcripts & indexes of marriages 1849-93 & burials 1846-1896; also Wesleyan Methodist baptisms 1873-92

Tansley

- Holy Trinity Church: indexes to baptism, marriage and burial registers 1840-1899
  freespace.virgin.net/denys.gaskell/tansley.html
  At Tansley

Tickenhall

- Marriages at Tickenhall, 1626 to 1812
  www.uk-genealogy.org.uk/england/Derbyshire/towns/t/Tickenhall/index.html
  Facsimile of the published Phillimore transcription

Tideswell

- The Feudal History of the County of Derby, volume 5, chapter 16: Parish Registers
  www.genuki.org.uk/big/eng/DBY/Yeatman/Volume5/Chapter16.html
  For Tideswell, 1635-1800

West Hallam

- Marriages at West Hallam, 1638 to 1812
  www.uk-genealogy.org.uk/england/Derbyshire/towns/w/WestHallam/Index.html
  Facsimile of the published Phillimore transcription

Whittington

- Whittington (Derbyshire) Deaths & Burials
  www.genuki.org.uk/big/eng/DBY/Whittington/Burials.html
  Index, 1813-1847

Willington

- Marriages at Willington, 1698 to 1812
  www.uk-genealogy.org.uk/england/Derbyshire/towns/w/Willington/index.html
  Facsimile of the published Phillimore transcription

- Willington 1698-1812: Brides
  homepage.ntlworld.com/sherwoodoutlaw/willingtonbride.htm
  Index. For an index of grooms, see **/willingtongroom.htm**

Winster

- Marriages at St. John the Baptist Church, Winster, Derbyshire, where either one or both parties were not 'of this parish'. Years covered this page 1681-1837
  winster-ancestry.com/stray-marriages-one.html

Wirksworth

- Wirksworth Parish Records 1600-1900
  www.wirksworth.org.uk
  Includes parish registers, 1608-1899, *etc.*

Woodville

- Woodville St. Stephens (formerly Wooden Box) Parish Page
  freepages.genealogy.rootsweb.com/~brett/woodville/woodville.htm
  Includes baptisms 1847-1908, marriages 1848-1900 & burials 1847-1941

- Woodville St. Stephens Baptisms 1847-1853
  freepages.genealogy.rootsweb.com/~brett/parregs/woodbap_a.htm
  Continued to 1872, with separate surname index, on 4 further pages. Also available (with continuation to 1908) as above

- Woodville St. Stephens Marriages 1848-1862
  freepages.genealogy.rootsweb.com/~brett/parregs/woodmar_a.htm
  Continued to 1881, with separate surname index, on 3 further pages. Also available (with continuation to 1900) as above

- Woodville St. Stephens Burials 1847-1862
  freepages.genealogy.rootsweb.com/~brett/parregs/woodbur_a.htm
  Continued to 1882, with separate index, on 3 further pages. Also available (with continuation to 1860) as above

Youlgreave

- Baptisms, Marriages and Burials at All Saints Church, Youlgreave
  www.genuki.org.uk/big/eng/DBY/Youlgreave/CDAllSaints.html
  Details of a CD

Durham

Civil Registration

See also Yorkshire (for Cleveland area)

- Births, Deaths, Marriages Registration
  www.durham.gov.uk/durham/usp.nsf/pws/registrar++registration+service
  Includes list of Church of England registers held by the Co. Durham Registration Service, details of a computerized index to the civil registers, and other information for family historians

- Registration Districts in Durham
  www.fhsc.org.uk/genuki/REG/dur.htm
  Between 1837 and 1930

- Durham County Record Office User Guide 1: A Brief Guide to Civil Registration
  www.durham.gov.uk/recordoffice/usp.nsf/lookup/pdfhandlists/$file/userguide01.pdf

- [St.Catherine's House Marriage Index, Jan-March, 1849. District 24. County Durham/Northumberland]
  www.cs.ncl.ac.uk/genuki/StCathsTranscriptions/CATH4924.TXT

Parish & Non-Parochial Registers: Introductory Pages & Lists

See also Northumberland, for registers in Newcastle upon Tyne

- Durham County Record Office. Handlist 2. Parish Registers
  www.durham.gov.uk/recordoffice/usp.nsf/lookup/pdfhandlists/$file/handlist02.pdf

- Church of England Parishes in Co. Durham
  www.durham.gov.uk/recordoffice/dro.nsf/web/parishes
  List of parishes with details of parish registers available at Durham Record Office

- Durham County Record Office Handlist 3: Modern Transcripts and Indexes (Church of England)
  www.durham.gov.uk/recordoffice/usp.nsf/lookup/pdfhandlists/$file/handlist03.pdf

- Durham County Record Office User Guide 7: Guide to Census and Parish Register Microfilms
  www.durham.gov.uk/recordoffice/usp.nsf/lookup/pdfhandlists/$file/userguide07.pdf

- Durham County Record Office. Handlist 1. Non-Conformist Church Registers
  www.durham.gov.uk/recordoffice/usp.nsf/lookup/pdfhandlists/$file/handlist01.pdf

- Durham County Record Office. Handlist 6. Modern Transcripts and Indexes (Non-conformist and Miscellaneous)
  www.durham.gov.uk/recordoffice/usp.nsf/lookup/pdfhandlists/$file/handlist06.pdf

- Tyne & Wear Archives User Guides
  www.thenortheast.com/archives/guides.html
  Includes guides to 'Parish Registers on Microfilm', 'Roman Catholic Registers', 'Methodist Registers', 'Registers of other denominations', *etc.* The area covered includes Gateshead, Newcastle, North Tyneside, South Tyneside and Sunderland

- Darlington Library Centre for Local Studies. Parish Registers
  www.darlington.gov.uk/dar_public/Documents/Education/Library/Parish%20Register%20Copy1.pdf

- Gateshead Council. Local Studies Department. Church Records: Microfilm & Transcripts
  www.genuki.org.uk/big/eng/DUR/GatesheadLib/register.html

- Durham
  www.sog.org.uk/prc/durham.html
  Parish registers, printed, typescript, etc., in the library of the Society of Genealogists

- Library Catalogue
  www.ndfhs.fsnet/co.uk/Catalogue.pdf
  Library catalogue of Northumberland & Durham Family History Society; includes many parish registers

- Northumberland & Durham Family History Society. Transcripts on Computer at Bolbec Hall. Part 1: Co. Durham
  www.ndfhs.fsnet.co.uk/TranscriptsDUR.html
  List of parish register transcripts

- Quaker Family History Society: Durham
  www.rootsweb.com/~engqfhs/Research/counties/durham.htm
  Notes on Quaker records

Indexes
- A Marriage Database for Northern England (the Joiner Marriage Index)
  website.lineone.net/~jjoiner/mindex/mindex.html
  Covers 442 parishes in Durham and North Yorkshire

- Parishes covered by Boyd's Marriage Index: Durham
  www.britishorigins.com/help/popup-aboutbo-bmi-countydetails.htm
  Click on 'Durham'

- County Durham Burial Index 1813-1837 (5% sample)
  www.cs.ncl.ac.uk/genuki/Transcriptions/DUR/BDUR.html

- Durham County Record Office Handlist 8: Parishes Indexed on International Genealogical Index and on Boyd's Marriage Index
  www.durham.gov.uk/recordoffice/usp.nsf/lookup/pdfhandlists/$file/handlist08.pdf

- IGI Batch Numbers for Durham, England
  freepages.genealogy.rootsweb.com/~hughwallis/IGIBatchNumbers/CountyDurham.htm

- Durham, England: Parish and Probate Records
  www.ancestry.com/search/db.aspx?dbid=5871
  Index to published registers *etc.*

- West Durham Database
  freespace.virgin.net/ron.nubley/
  Offline index to over 750,000 events pre-1851

- Durham Records Online
  www.durhamrecordsonline.com/
  Index to parish registers of Easington and district; pay per view site

Miscellaneous
- Executions at Durham 1732-1909
  www.genuki.org.uk/big/eng/DUR/D_Executions.html

Publications
- Northfiche: Parish Register Transcripts & Indexes: Durham & Cumberland
  www.jwillans.freeserve.co.uk/northfic.html
  Lists of transcripts *etc.,* on fiche for sale

- Original Indexes
  www.original-indexes.demon.co.uk/
  Lists parish registers *etc.,* available on fiche for Co. Durham and Northumberland

- Publications Available from the Cleveland, North Yorkshire and South Durham Family History Society
  www.clevelandfhs.org.uk/Publications.htm
  Includes parish register transcriptions for the Cleveland area of Co. Durham and Yorkshire

- Durham: Lindenbridge Publications & Research Services
  lindenbridge.pubs.tripod.com/lindenbridgepublications/
  Many fiche for sale relating to the South Shields area

Auckland St. Helen
- Marriages from the Auckland St. Helen Registers (1593-1837)
  www.cs.ncl_ac.uk/genuki/Transcriptions/DUR/ASH.html

Aycliffe
- Marriages from the Aycliffe Registers (1560-1837)
  www.cs.ncl.ac.uk/genuki/Transcriptions/DUR/AYC.html

Barnard Castle
- Barnard Castle Baptisms 1813-1837
  www.cs.ncl.ac.uk/Transcriptions/DUR/XBAR_A-C.html
  Index, continued on 3 further pages

- Barnard Castle Burials 1813-1837
  www.cs.ncl.ac.uk/genuki/Transcriptions/DUR/BBAR_A-K.html
  Index, completed at **/BBAR_L-Y.html**

Bishop Middleham

- Marriages from the Bishop Middleham Registers (1559-1837)
  www.cs.ncl.ac.uk/genuki/Transcriptions/BMI.html

Bishopton

- Marriages from the Bishopton Registers (1653-1837)
  www.cs.ncl.ac.uk/genuki/Transcriptions/DUR/BIS.html

Bishopwearmouth

- Marriages from the Bishopwearmouth Registers (1813-1823)
  www.cs.ncl.ac.uk/genuki/Transcriptions/DUR/BWM1813.html
  Continued for 1824-31 at **/BWM1824.html** and for 1832-7 at **/BWM1832.html**

Blackhill Cemetery

- Grave Text
  www.gravetext.co.uk
  Database of burial records for Blackhill Cemetery. Pay per view site

Boldon

- Marriages from the Boldon Registers (1573-1837)
  www.cs.ncl.ac.uk/genuki/Transcriptions/DUR/BOL.html

Castle Eden

- Marriages from the Castle Eden registers (1698-1837)
  www.cs.ncl.ac.uk/genuki/Transcriptions/DUR/CED.html

Chester le Street

- Marriages from the Chester le Street registers (1582-1699)
  www.cs.ncl.ac.uk/genuki/Transcriptions/DUR/CLS1582.gtml
  Continued as follows:
  1700-1749 **CLS1700.html** 1750-1774 **CLS1750.html**
  1775-1799 **CLS1775.html** 1800-1837 **CLS1800.html**

Cockfield

- Cockfield Baptisms 1813-1838
  www.cs.ncl.ac.uk/genuki/Transcriptions/DUR/XCOC.html

- Marriages from the Cockfield Registers (1579-1837)
  www.cs.ncl.ac.uk/genuki/Transcriptions/DUR/COC.html

- Cockfield Burials 1807-1840
  www.cs.ncl.ac.uk/genuki/Transcriptions/DUR/BCOC.html

Cold Hesledon

See Seaham

Coniscliffe

- Marriages from the Coniscliffe Registers (1590-1837)
  www.cs.ncl.ac.uk/genuki/Transcriptions/DUR/Coniscliffe.html

Croxdale

- Croxdale Baptisms 1813-1893
  www.genuki.org.uk/big/eng/DUR/CroxdaleBap.html

- Marriages from the Croxdale Registers (1732-1837)
  www.cs.ncl.ac.uk/genuki/Transcriptions/DUR/CRO.html

Dalton le Dale

See also Seaham

- Marriages from the Dalton le Dale Registers (1653-1837)
  www.cs.acl.ac.uk/genuki/Transcriptions/DUR/DLD.html

Denton

- Marriages from the Denton Registers (1673-1837)
  www.cs.ncl.ac.uk/genuki/Transcriptions/DUR/DEN.html

Durham

- Marriages from the Durham Cathedral Registers (1609-1837)
  www.css.ncl.ac.uk/genuki/Transcriptions/DUR/DCA.html

- Marriages from the Durham St. Margaret Registers (1558-1739)
  www.cs.ncl.ac.uk/genuki/Transcriptions/DUR/DSM.html
  Continued for 1740-1837 at **/DSM1740.html**

- Marriages from the Durham St. Mary-le-Bow Registers (1571-1837)
  www.cs.ncl.ac.uk/genuki/Transcriptions/DUR/DSB.html

- Marriages from the Durham St. Mary South Bailey Registers (1559-1837)
  www.cs.ncl.ac.uk/genuki/Transcriptions/DUR/DSL.html

- Marriages from the Durham St. Nicholas Registers (1540-1719)
  www.cs.ncl.ac.uk/genuki/Transcriptions/DUR/DSN.html
  Continued for 1720-1837 at **DSN1720.html**

- Marriages from the Durham St. Oswald Registers (1538-1734)
  www.cs.ncl.ac.uk/genuki/Transcriptions/DUR/DSO.html
  Continued for 1735-1837 at **/DSO1735.html**

Easington
- Marriages from the Easington Registers (1570-1837)
  www.cs.ncl.ac.uk/genuki/Transcriptions/DUR/EAS.html

Ebchester
- Marriages from the Ebchester Registers (1619-1837)
  www.cs.ncl.ac.uk/genuki/Transcriptions/DUR/EBC.html

Edmundbyers
- Marriages from the Edmundbyers Registers (1764-1837)
  www.cs.ncl.ac.uk/genuki/Transcriptions/DUR/EDM.html

- Edmundbyers Burials 1813-1837
  www.cs.ncl.ac.uk/genuki/DUR/BEDM.html
  Index

Egglescliffe
- Marriages from the Egglescliffe Registers (1540-1837)
  www.cs.ncl.ac.uk/genuki/Transcriptions/DUR/EGG.html

Egglestone
- Egglestone Baptisms 1795-1812
  www.cs.ncl.ac.uk/Transcriptions/DUR/XEGT1795.html
  Index. Continued for 1813-1837 at **/XEGT.html**

- Egglestone Burials 1796-1840
  www.cs.ncl.ac.uk/genuki/Transcriptions/DUR/BEGT.html
  Index

Elwick Hall
- Marriages from the Elwick Hall Registers (1592-1837)
  www.cs.ncl.ac.uk/genuki/Transcriptions/DUR/ELW.html

Embleton
- Marriages from the Embleton Registers (1653-1752)
  www.cs.ncl.ac.uk/genuki/Transcriptions/DUR/EMN.html

Escomb
- Marriages from the Escombe Registers (1543-1837)
  www.cs.ncl.ac.uk/genuki/Transcriptions/DUR/ESC.html

Esh
- Marriages from the Esh Registers (1570-1837)
  www.cs.ncl.ac.uk/genuki/Transcriptions/DUR/ESH.html

Gainford
- Marriages from the Gainford Registers (1569-1719)
  www.cs.ncl.ac.uk/genuki/Transcriptions/DUR/GAI/html
  Continued for 1720-1837 at **/GAI1720.html**

Gateshead
- Marriages from the Gateshead Registers (1558-1837)
  www.cs.ncl.ac.uk/genuki/Transcriptions/DUR/GAT1558.html
  Actually only to 1597 on this page. Continued as follows:

1600-1699	**/GAT1600.html**	1700-1724	**/GAT1700.html**
1725-1749	**/GAT1725.html**	1750-1779	**/GAT1750.html**
1780-1799	**/GAT1780.html**	1800-1819	**/GAT1800.html**
1820-1837	**/GAT1820.html**		

- Victims of the 1854 Fire and Explosion in Gateshead
  www.genuki.org.uk/big/eng/DUR/GreatFire/index.html

Gateshead Fell
- Gateshead Fell Baptisms 1825-1837
  www.cs.ncl.ac.uk/Transcriptions/DUR/XGAF.html

- Marriages from the Gateshead Fell Registers (1825-1837)
  www.cs.ncl.ac.uk/genuki/Transcriptions/DUR/GAF.html

Great Lumley
- Notebook of Richard Nelson (1825-1911), first sexton of Great Lumley Parish Church
  www.genuki.org.uk/big/eng/DUR/Transcriptions/RNelson.htm
  Includes burials and marriages, 1866-71

Great Stainton

- Marriages from the Great Stainton registers (1561-1837)
  www.cs.ncl.ac.uk/genuki/Transcriptions/DUR/GST.html

Greatham

- Marriages from the Greatham Registers (1564-1837)
  www.cs.ncl.ac.uk/genuki/Transcriptions/DUR/GRE.html

Grindon

- Marriages from the Grindon registers (1565-1837)
  www.cs.ncl.ac.uk/genuki/Transcriptions/DUR/GRI.html

Hamsterley

- Marriages from the Hamsterley Registers (1580-1837)
  www.cs.ncl.ac.uk/genuki/Transcriptions/DUR/HAM.html

Hartlepool

- Hartlepool Parish Church Registers
  hometown.aol.com/bertw181/hartlepool.html
  Off-line printouts of index entries

Hawthorn

See Seaham

Heathery Cleugh

- Marriages from the Heathery Cleugh Registers (1828-1837)
  www.cs.ncl.ac.uk/genuki/Transcriptions/DUR/HCL.html

- Heathery Cleugh Burials 1824-1837
  www.cs.ncl.ac.uk/Transcriptions/DUR/BHCL.html
  Index

Heighington

- Marriages from the Heighington Registers (1570-1837)
  www.cs.ncl.ac.uk/genuki/Transcriptions/DUR/HEI.html

Heworth

- Marriages from the Heworth Registers (1696-1774)
  www.cs.ncl.ac.uk/genuki/Transcriptions/DUR/HEW.html
  Continued for 1775-1837 at **/HEW1775.html**

Hetton le Hole

- Marriages from the Hetton-le-Hole Registers (1832-1837)
  www.cs.ncl.ac.uk/genuki/Transcriptions/DUR/HLH.html

Houghton le Spring

- Marriages from the Houghton-le-Spring Registers (1563-1699)
  www.cs.ncl.ac.uk/Transcriptions/DUR/HSP1563.html
  Continued as follows:
  1700-1749 **/HSP1700.html** 1750-1799 **/HSP1750.html**
  1800-1824 **/HSP1800.html** 1825-1837 **/HSP1825.html**

Hunstanworth

- Marriages from the Hunstanworth Registers (1770-1837)
  www.cs.ncl.ac.uk/Transcriptions/DUR/HUN.html

- Hunstanworth Burials 1813-1837
  www.cs.ncl.ac.uk/Transcriptions/DUR/BHUN.html

Hurworth

- Marriages from the Hurworth Registers (1559-1837)
  www.cs.ncl.ac.uk/Transcriptions/DUR/HUR.html

Jarrow

- Marriages from the Registers of Jarrow St. Mark (1896-1948)
  www.cs.ncl.ac.uk/Transcriptions/DUR/MJARSM.html

- Marriages from the Jarrow Registers (1813-1824)
  www.cs.ncl.ac.uk/Transcriptions/DUR/MJAR1813.html
  St. Paul's. Continued for 1825-1837 at **/MJAR1825.html**

- Marriages from the Registers of Jarrow St. Peter (1881-1923)
  www.cs.ncl.ac.uk/Transcriptions/DUR/MJARSP.html

Jarrow Grange

- Marriages from the Registers of Jarrow Grange Christ Church (1869-1900)
  www.cs.ncl.ac.uk/Transcriptions/DUR/MJARCC.html

- Marriages from the Registers of Jarrow Grange Good Shepherd (1893-1949)
  www.cs.ncl.ac.uk/Transcriptions/DUR/MJARGS.html

Kelloe

- Marriages from the Kelloe Registers (1693-1837)
  www.cs.ncl.ac.uk/Transcriptions/DUR/KEL.html

Lamesley

- Index to Lamesley Baptism Register 1730-1797
  www.cs.ncl.ac.uk/Transcriptions/DUR/XLAM-AF.html
  Continued at **/XLAM-GP.html** and **/XLAM-RY.html**
- Marriages from the Lamesley Registers (1689-1837)
  www.cs.ncl.ac.uk/Transcriptions/DUR/LAM.html

Long Newton

- Marriages from the Long Newton Registers (1564-1837)
  www.cs.ncl.ac.uk/Transcriptions/DUR/LON.html

Medomsley

- Marriages from the Medomsley Registers (1608-1837)
  www.cs.ncl.ac.uk/Transcriptions/DUR/MED.html

Merrington

- Marriages from the Merrington Registers (1579-1837)
  www.cs.ncl.ac.uk/Transcriptions/DUR/MER.html

Middleton in Teesdale

- Middleton in Teesdale Baptisms 1753-1841
  www.cs.ncl.ac.uk/genuki/Transcriptions/DUR/XMTD__A.html
  Alphabetical index. Continued on 7 further pages
- Middleton in Teesdale Baptisms 1813-1841
  www.cs.ncl.ac.uk/Transcriptions/DUR/XMTD__A-E.html
  Alphabetical index. Several further pages
- Marriages from the Middleton-in-Teesdale Registers (1621-1784)
  www.cs.ncl.ac.uk/Transcriptions/DUR/MTD.html
  Continued for 1785-1837 at **/MTD1785.html**
- Middleton in Teesdale Burials 1753-1840
  www.cs.ncl.ac.uk/genuki/Transcriptions/DUR/BMDT-AF.html
  Alphabetical index. Continued at **/BMDT-GR.html** and **/BMDT-SW.html**

Middleton St. George

- Marriages from the Middleton St. George Registers (1616-1837)
  www.cs.ncl.ac.uk/Transcriptions/DUR/MSG.html

Monk Hesledon

- Marriages from the Monk Hesledon Registers (1592-1837)
  www.cs.ncl.ac.uk/Transcriptions/DUR/MHE.html

Monkwearmouth

- Marriages from the Monkwearmouth Registers (1583-1799)
  www.cs.ncl.ac.uk/Transcriptions/DUR/MWM1583.html
  Continued as follows:

1800-1812	**/MWM1800.html**	1813-1826	**/MWM1813/html**
1825-1837	**/MWM1825.html**	1827-1837	**/MWM1827.html**

Muggleswick

- Marriages from the Muggleswick Registers (1755-1837)
  www.cs.ncl.ac.uk/Transcriptions/DUR/MUG.html
  Continued for 1837-1846 at **/MMUG.html**
- Muggleswick Burials 1813-1837
  www.cs.ncl.ac.uk/genuki/Transcriptions/DUR/BMUG.html
  Index

Murton

See Seaham

New Seaham

See Seaham

Old Seaham

See Seaham

Penshaw

- Marriages from the Penshaw Registers (1754-1837)
  www.cs.ncl.ac.uk/Transcriptions/DUR/PEN.html

Pittington

- Marriages from the Pittington Registers (1575-1837)
  www.cs.ncl.ac.uk/Transcriptions/DUR/PIT.html

Redmarshall

- Marriages from the Redmarshall Registers (1560-1837)
  www.cs.ncl.ac.uk/Transcriptions/DUR/RED.html

Ryton

- Marriages from the Ryton Registers (1581-1699)
  www.cs.ncl.ac.uk/Transcriptions/DUR/RYT1581.html
  Continued as follows:

1700-1749	**/RYT1700.html**	1750-1779	**/RYT1750.html**
1780-1812	**/RYT1780.html**	1800-1837	**/RYT1800.html**
1813-1837	**/RYT1813.html**		

Satley

- Marriages from the Satley Registers (1560-1837)
  www.cs.ncl.ac.uk/Transcriptions/DUR/SAT.html

Seaham

- Marriages from the Seaham Registers (1652-1837)
  www.cs.ncl.ac.uk/Transcriptions/DUR/SEA.html

Sedgefield

- Marriages from the Sedgefield Registers (1581-1729)
  www.cs.ncl.ac.uk/Transcriptions/DUR/SED.html
  Continued for 1730-1837 at **/SED1730.html**

Sherburn Hospital

- Marriages from the Sherburn Hospital Registers (1695-1837)
  www.cs.ncl.ac.uk/genuki/Transcriptions/DUR/SHO.html

Shildon

- Marriages from the Shildon Registers (1834-1837)
  www.cs.ncl.ac.uk/Transcriptions/DUR/SHI.html

Sockburn

- Marriages from the Sockburn Registers (1580-1837)
  www.cs.ncl.ac.uk/Transcriptions/DUR/SOC.html

South Shields

- Marriages from the Registers of South Shields St. Aiden (1888-1910)
  www.cs.ncl.ac.uk/Transcriptions/DUR/MSSHSA.html

- Marriages from the South Shields St. Hilda Registers (1653-1699)
  www.cs.ncl.ac.uk/Transcriptions/DUR/SSH1653.html
  Continued as follows:

1700-1749	**/SSH1700.html**	1750-1779	**/SSH1750.html**
1780-1799	**/SSH1780.html**	1800-1812	**/SSH1800.html**
1813-1824	**/SSH1813.html**	1825-1837	**/SSH1825.html**
1837-1844	**/MSSH1837.html**	1845-1850	**/MSSH1845.html**
1851-1858	**/MSSH1851.html**	1859-1868	**/MSSH1859.html**
1869-1880	**/MSSH1869.html**	1881-1901	**/MSSH1881.html**

- Marriages from the Registers of South Shields St. Jude (1886-1914)
  www.cs.ncl.ac.uk/Transcriptions/DUR/MSSHSJ.html
- Marriages from the Registers of South Shields St. Michael (1882-1889)
  www.cs.ncl.ac.uk/Transcriptions/DUR/MSSHSM1882.html
  Continued for 1900-1908 at **/MSSHSM1900.html**
- South Shields Society of Friends: Burials 1673-1697
  www.cs.ncl.ac.uk/genuki/Transcriptions/DUR/BSSH-SoF.html
  From *Archaeologia Aeliana* N.S. **16**(1), 1894

Spennymoor

- Derek Boy's Index to Marriage Registers of St. Paul's, Spennymoor, 1863-1914
  www.cs.ncl.ac.uk/genuki/Transcriptions/DUR/SpennyA-J.html

Staindrop

- Staindrop Baptisms 1813-1838
  www.cs.ncl.ac.uk/Transcriptions/DUR/XSTD_A-J.html
  Alphabetical index. Continued at **/XSTD_K-Y.html**
- Marriages from the Staindrop Registers (1626-1764)
  www.cs.ncl.ac.uk/Transcriptions/DUR/STD.html
  Continued for 1765-1837 at **/STD1765.html**
- Staindrop Burials 1813-1840
  www.cs.ncl.ac.uk/genuki/Transcriptions/DUR/BSTD.html
  Index

Stanhope

- Marriages from the Stanhope Registers (1613-1749)
  www.cs.ncl.ac.uk/Transcriptions/DUR/STP1613.html
  Continued as follows:

1750-1799	**/STP1750.html**	1800-1837	**/STP1800.html**

- Stanhope Burial Register 1854-1905
  www.cs.ncl.ac.uk/genuki/Transcriptions/DUR/BSTP-AG.html
  Continued at **/BSTP-HP.html** & **/BSTP-RY.html**

Stockton on Tees
- Stockton on Tees Baptisms 1637-1780
  www.cs.ncl.ac.uk/Transcriptions/DUR/XSTO__A-B.html
  Alphabetical index. Continued on 6 further pages.

- Stockton St. James 1868-1910
  homepages.rootsweb.com/~mwi/stockton.txt
  Marriages

Sunderland
- Marriages from the Sunderland Registers (1719-1749)
  www.cs.ncl.ac.uk/Transcriptions/DUR/SUN1719.html
  Continued as follows:

1750-1764	**/SUN1750.html**	1765-1774	**/SUN1765.html**
1775-1784	**/SUN1775.html**	1785-1799	**/SUN1785.html**
1800-1814	**/SUN1800.html**	1815-1824	**/SUN1815.html**
1825-1829	**/SUN1825.html**	1830-1837	**/SUN1830.html**

- Victims of the Victoria Hall Calamity
  www.genuki.org.uk/big/eng/DUR/Sunderland/VictoriaHall.html
  Lists victims of a Sunderland tragedy in 1883

Trimdon
- Marriages from the Trimdon Registers (1720-1837)
  www.cs.ncl.ac.uk/Transcriptions/DUR/TRI.html

Washington
- Marriages from the Washington Registers (1603-1837)
  www.cs.ncl.ac.uk/Transcriptions/DUR/WAS.html

Weardale St. John
See also Wolsingham

- Marriages from the St. John's Chapel (Weardale) Registers (1828-1837)
  www.cs.ncl.ac.uk/Transcriptions/DUR/SJC.html

West Baldon
- West Boldon Society of Friends Burials 1657-1682
  www.cs.ncl.ac.uk/genuki/BBOL-Sof.html
  From *Archaeologia Aeliana* N.S. **16**(1), 1894

West Rainton
- Marriages from the West Rainton Registers (1827-1837)
  www.cs.ncl.ac.uk/Transcriptions/DUR/WRA.html

Whickham
- Marriages from the Whickham Registers (1534-1654)
  www.cs.ncl.ac.uk/Transcriptions/DUR/WHK1579.html
  Continued as follows:

1655-1724	**/WHK1655.html**	1725-1774	**/WHK1725.html**
1775-1812	**/WHK1775.html**	1813-1837	**/WHK1813.html**

Whitburn
- Whitburn Baptisms 1813-1839
  www.cs.ncl.ac.uk/Transcriptions/DUR/XWBN.html

- Marriages from the Whitburn Registers (1579-1837)
  www.cs.ncl.ac.uk/Transcriptions/DUR/WBN.html

Whitworth
- Marriages from the Whitworth Registers 1754-1837
  www.cs.ncl.ac.uk/Transcriptions/DUR/MWHW.html

Whorlton
- Whorlton Baptisms 1841-1899
  www.cs.ncl.ac.uk/Transcriptions/DUR/XWHO.html
  Index

- Marriages from the Whorlton Registers (1713-1837)
  www.cs.ncl.ac.uk/Transcriptions/DUR/WHO.html

- Whorlton Burials 1813-1899
  www.cs.ncl.ac.uk/Transcriptions/DUR/BWHO.html
  Index

Winlaton
- Marriages from the Winlaton Registers (1833-1837)
  www.cs.ncl.ac.uk/Transcriptions/DUR/MWinlaton.html

Winston

- Winstone Baptisms 1813-1840
  www.cs.ncl.ac.uk/Transcriptions/DUR/XWIS.html
  Index

- Marriages from the Winston Registers (1716-1837)
  www.cs.ncl.ac.uk/Transcriptions/DUR/WIS.html

- Winston Burials 1814-1840
  www.cs.ncl.ac.uk/Transcriptions/DUR/BWIS.html
  Index

Witton Gilbert

- Marriages from the Witton Gilbert Registers (1568-1837)
  www.cs.ncl.ac.uk/Transcriptions/DUR/WIT.html

Witton le Wear

- Marriages from the Witton le Wear Registers (1558-1837)
  www.cs.ncl.ac.uk/Transcriptions/DUR/WLW.html

Wolsingham

- Wolsingham and Weardale Chapel Baptisms 1813-1827
  website.lineone.net/~pjoiner/genuki/DUR/Wolsingham/WOL.html

Essex

Civil Registration

- Registration Districts in Essex
  www.fhsc.org.uk/genuki/REG/ess.htm
  Between 1837 and 1930

- The St. Catherine's Marriage Index October/November/December 1839: [Essex and S. Suffolk]
  www.cs.ncl.ac.uk/genuki/StCathsTranscriptions/
  Includes transcripts of civil registration indexes covering Essex and South Suffolk, 1839-44 and 1849

Parish & Non-Parochial Registers: Introductory Pages & Lists

- Essex
  www.sog.org.uk/prc/ess.html
  Parish registers, printed, typescript, etc., in the library of the Society of Genealogists

- Quaker Family History Society: Essex
  www.rootsweb.com/~engqfhs/Research/counties/essex.htm
  Notes on Quaker records

Indexes

- Essex Villages
  www.essexvillages.net
  Includes indexes to parish registers

- Essex Baptism Index 1780-1840
  www.nivek-systems.co.uk/genuki/ESS/ESS.baptisms.html

- Marriages
  www.nivek-systems.co.uk/genuki/ESS/ESS.marriages.html
  Notes on Essex marriage indexes

- Parishes covered by Boyd's Marriage Index: Essex
  www.britishorigins.com/help/popup-aboutbo-bmi-countydetails.htm
  Click on 'Essex'

- Some Marriage Entries from Boyd's Index for Essex
  freepages.genealogy.rootsweb.com/~boydsindex/Boydsindex.htm

- National Burial Index (Essex SFH)
  www.familyhistoryonline.co.uk/database/NBIEssexSFH.shtml
  Pay per view

- Essex Burials 1813-1865
  www.nivek-systems.co.uk/genuki/ESS/ESS.burials.html
  Index

- IGI Batch Numbers for Essex, England
  freepages.genealogy.rootsweb.com/~hughwallis/IGIBatchNumbers/CountyEssex.htm

- Essex, England, Parish and Probate Records
  www.ancestry.com/search/db/aspx?dbid=5872
  Index to published registers

Publications

- The East of London F.H.S. Store
  www.eolfhs.org.uk/eolstore
  Includes parish register transcripts and indexes relating to Essex and Middlesex

Beaumont

- An Index to the Registers of Beaumont, Essex, U.K.
  www.essexpast.co.uk/beaumont/bmntintro.html
  Based on Crisp's transcript published in 1899

Earls Colne

- Earls Colne, Essex: Records of an English Village 1375-1854
  linux02.lib.cam.ac.uk/earlscolne/
  Baptisms, 1560-1854; marriages 1559-1853; burials 1559-1854. Also includes events in other parishes relating to Earls Colne, and a vast amount of other data

Haverhill

- Haverhill Cemetery Burial Records
  www.haverhill-uk.com/genealogy/cemetery/index.shtml
  Searchable database, 1867-1950. Also includes Hundon Chapel Burials

Kelvedon Hatch

- The History of Kelvedon Hatch: St. Nicholas Church
  www.historyhouse.co.uk/stnicholas.html
  Marriages 1837-1898; burials 1813-1897

Mount Bures

- Mount Bures
  mysite.wanadoo-members.co.uk/Mountbures
  Baptisms 1668-1751 & 1818-39; marriages 1668-1714; burials 1668-1714 & 1813-1957. Continued at **/Mount-Bures2**

Steeple Bumpstead

- Steeple Bumpstead Baptisms, 1676-1907
  www.haverhill-uk.com/genealogy/baptisms/steeple_bumpstead_baptsms.shtml

- Steeple Bumpstead Marriages listed by Female Name
  www.haverhill-uk.com/genealogy/marriages/sb_marriages_female.shtml
  For index to male names see **/sb_marriages_male.shtml**

Tendring Hundred

- Demographic History of a Group of Nine Parishes in the Tendring Hundred, Essex 1533-1838 (study number 978)
  hds.essex.ac.uk/studybrowse/showabstract.php?sn=978
  See also **=9887**
  Includes registers of Harwich, Dovercourt, Wrabness, Ramsey, Wix, Tendring, Great Oakley, Little Oakley and Beaumont cum Moze

Wakes Colne

- Wakes Colne
  mysite.wanadoo-members.co.uk/www.colnedatabase.co/
  Marriages 1694-1700 & 1813-93; burials 1813-87

- Wakes Colne
  mysite.wanadoo-members.co.uk/Wakes_Colne_Continued
  Baptisms 1700-1710 & 1857-69; marriages 1700-1710; burials 1700-1710 & 1764-1812

Hertfordshire

Civil Registration

- Births, Marriages and Deaths
  www.hertsdirect.org/publicservs/register/
  Hertfordshire civil registration

- Registration Districts in Hertfordshire
  www.fhsc.org.uk/genuki/REG.hrt.htm
  Between 1837 and 1930

Parish & Non-Parochial Registers: Introductory Pages and Lists

- Parish Registers
  www.hertsdirect.org/libsleisure/heritage1/HALS/whatgot/parregs/
  Includes lists of registers in Hertfordshire libraries and archives

- Non-conformist Registers
  www.her5tsdirect.org/libsleisure/heritage1/HALS/whatgot/noncon
  Includes list of registers at Hertfordshire Archives Local Studies

- Hertfordshire
  www.sog.org.uk/prc/hertfordshire.html
  Parish registers, printed, typescript, *etc.,* in the library of the Society of Genealogists

- Quaker Family History Society: Hertfordshire
  www.rootsweb.com/~engqfhs/Research/counties/hertford.htm
  Notes on Quaker records

Indexes

- National Burial Index (Hertfordshire F.H.S.)
  www.familyhistoryonline.co.uk/database/NBIHertfordshireFHS.shtml
  Pay per view

- IGI Batch Numbers for Hertford, England
  freepages.genealogy.rootsweb.com/~hughwallis/IGIBatchNumbers/CountyHertford.htm

- Hertfordshire, England, Parish and Probate Records
  www.ancestry.com/search/db.aspx?dbid=5885
  Index to published registers

Bovingdon

- Transcribed documents relating to Bovingdon, Hertfordshire
  www.geocities.com/mellowsbrown/tranlist.html
  Lookups offered in the parish registers, monumental inscriptions *etc.*

Cheshunt

- Cheshunt Cemetery: Adath Yisroel Burial Society Records
  www.jgsgb.org.uk/bury01.shtml
  Index to records of a Jewish cemetery

Little Munden

- Genealogy
  www.mundens.net/genealogy/
  Includes brief notes on 17-18th c. registers, *etc.*

Huntingdonshire

Civil Registration

- Registration Districts in Huntingdon
  www.fhsc.org.uk/genuki/REG/hun.htm
  Between 1837 and 1930

Parish & Non-Parochial Registers: Introductory Pages & Lists

- Summary of Documentary and Library Holdings in the Huntingdon County Record Office
  www.genuki.org.uk/big/eng/HUN/RecordOffice.html
  Includes brief notes on registers *etc.*
- Microfilm Holdings of Parish Registers & Bishops Transcripts at the County Record Office, Huntingdon
  www.genuki.org.uk/big/eng/CAM/HuntingdonRecordOfficeMicrofilmHoldings.html
- Huntingdonshire
  www.sog.org.uk/prc/huntingdonshire.html
  Parish registers, printed, typescript, *etc.,* in the library of the Society of Genealogists
- Quaker Family History Society: Huntingdonshire
  www.rootsweb.com/~engqfhs/Research/counties/hunts.htm
  Notes on Quaker records

Indexes

- National Burial Index (Huntingdonshire F.H.S.)
  www.familyhistoryonline.co.uk/database/NBIHuntsFHS.shtml
  Pay per view
- IGI Batch Numbers for Huntingdon, England
  freepages.genealogy.rootsweb.com/~hughwallis/IGIBatchNumbers/CountyHuntingdon.htm

Publications

- Huntingdonshire Family History Society bookstall
  www.hunts.fhs.org.uk/Pubs.html
  Includes many parish registers, monumental inscriptions, *etc.* for sale

Eaton Socon

- Eaton Socon Burials 1813-1840
  www.rootsweb.com/~enghun/Transcriptions/EatonSoconBurials1813-1840/

Great Gidding

- Great Gidding Parish Register Extracts
  freepages.genealogy.rootsweb.com/~maureenbryson/id58.htm
  Selected surnames only

Little Gidding

See Steeple Gidding

Steeple Gidding

- Steeple Gidding and Little Gidding Parish Register Extracts
  freepages.genealogy.rootsweb.com/~maureenbryson/id63.htm
  Selected surnames only

Upwood

- Upwood Parish Register Extracts, Wills, Misc. Records
  freepages.genealogy.rootsweb.com/~maureenbryson/id64.htm
  Selected surnames only

Winwick

- Winwick Parish Register Extracts
  freepages.genealogy.rootsweb.com/~maureenbryson/id65.htm
  Selected surnames only, 17-19th c.

Isle of Man

Parish & Non-Parochial Registers; Introductory Pages & Lists
See also Cumberland

- Parish Records
  www.isle-of-man.com/manxnotebook/famhist/genealgy/church.htm
  Isle of Man registers; includes a collection of extracts

- Isle of Man
  www.sog.org.uk/prc/isleofman.html
  Parish registers, printed, typescript, *etc.,* in the library of the Society of Genealogists

- Quaker Family History Society: Isle of Man
  www.rootsweb.com/~engqfhs/Research/counties/man.htm
  Notes on Quaker records

Indexes
- IGI Batch Numbers for Isle of Man, England
  freepages.genealogy.rootsweb.com/~hughwallis/IGIBatchNumbers/CountyIsle_of_Man.htm

Publications
- Isle of Man Family History Society Publications
  www.isle-of-man.com/interests/genealogy/fhs/fhspub.shtml
  Includes burial registers *etc.*

Andreas
- Extracts from Andreas Parish Register
  www.isle-of-man.com/manxnotebook/parishes/as/preg.htm
  Includes marriages, 1655-85

Ballaugh
- Extracts from Ballaugh Parish Registers
  www.isle-of-man.com/manxnotebook/parishes/bh/regs.htm

- Notes from the Registers: the Parish of Ballaugh
  www.isle-of-man.com/manxnotesbook/manxnb/v02p055.htm

Braddon
- Parish of Braddan
  www.isle-of-man.com/manxnotebook/parishes/bn/regs.htm
  Brief extracts from the parish register

German
- Extract from German Vestry Book
  www.isle-of-man.com/manxnotebook/parishes/gn/preg.htm
  Includes brief notes on burials

Kirk Michael
- Notes on the Parish Registers of Kirk Michael, Isle of Mann
  www.isle-of-man.com/manxnotesbook/iomnhas/lm1p003.htm
  Brief discussion

Kirk Onchan
- The Kirk Onchan Registers
  www.isle-of-man.com/manxnotebook/parishes/on/onreg.htm
  Brief discussion with extracts

Lezayre
- Extracts from Lezayre Parish Registers
  www.isle-of-man.com/manxnotebook/parishes/le/regs.htm
  Covers 1696-1709

Lonan
- The Parish of Lonan
  www.isle-of-man.com/manxnotebook/parishes/ln/lnreg.htm
  Brief notes from the register

Malew
- Notes from the Registers: the Parish of Malew
  www.isle-of-man.com/manxnotebook/manxnb/v06p072.htm
  Brief extracts

Marown
- Extracts from the Parish Register
  www.isle-of-man.com/manxnotebook/parishes/mn/pr.htm
  Of Marown. Brief

Maughold

- The Parish of Maughold
  www.isle-of-man.com/manxnotebook/parishes/md/mdreg.htm
  Brief extracts from the parish register

Rushen

- Rushen Parish Church, with extracts from old parish books
  www.isle-of-man.com/manxnotebook/parishes/rn/preg.htm
  Brief discussion with extracts

Santan

- Santan Parish Registers
  www.isle-of-man.com/manxnotebook/parishes/sn/preg.htm
  Baptisms 1690-1717; burials 1656-1850. Incomplete?

Lancashire

Civil Registration

- Lancashire BMD: Births, Marriages and Deaths on the Internet
  www.lancashirebmd.org.uk
  Index to civil registers. Important

- Registration Districts in Lancashire
  www.fhsc.org.uk/genuki/REG/lan.htm
  Between 1837 and 1930

- [St. Catherine's House Marriage Index, Jan-March, 1849. District 20. Lancashire]
  www.cs.ncl.ac.uk/genuki/StCathsTranscriptions/CATH4920.TXT

- [St. Catherine's House Marriage Index, Jan-March, 1849. District 21. Lancashire]
  www.cs.ncl.ac.uk/genuki/StCathsTranscriptions/CATH4921.TXT

Parish & Non-Parish Registers: Introductory Pages & Lists

- Lancashire County Library: Library Services: Local Studies: Parish Registers
  www.lancashire.gov.uk/libraries/services/local/parish.asp
  Brief introduction

- Parish Registers held at Crosby Library
  freepages.genealogy.rootsweb.com/~hibernia/seflib.htm

- Knowsley Library Service: Parish Registers
  www.knowsley.gov.uk/leisure/libraries/services/localhistory/parish.html
  List of published and fiched registers held

- Tracing Your Family History at Knowsley Libraries: Cemetery Records
  www.knowsley.gov.uk/leisure/libraries/services/local/cem.html
  List of published and fiched registers held

- Family History in Manchester
  www.manchester.gov.uk/libraries/arls/famhist.htm
  Includes notes on, and lists of, 'Church of England Registers', 'Non-conformist, Catholic, and Jewish Records', and 'Cemetery Records and Monumental Inscriptions', *etc.,* at Manchester Public Library

- Records of Roman Catholic Churches held at the Liverpool Record Office
  freepages.genealogy.rootsweb.com/~hibernia/rchurchrec.html

- Liverpool Area Roman Catholic Registers on Microfilm at the Lancashire Record Office
  freepages.genealogy.rootsweb.com/~hibernia/rcromla.htm

- Roman Catholic Registers on Microfilm at the Liverpool Record Office
  freepages.genealogy.rootsweb.com/~hibernia/rcromlv.htm

- Parish Registers held at Oldham Local Studies and Archives
  www.oldham.gov.uk/community/local_studies_and_archives/parish-registers.htm

- Lancashire
  www.sog.org.uk/prc/lancashire.html
  Parish registers, printed, typescript, etc., in the library of the Society of Genealogists

- Quaker Family History Society: Lancashire
  www.rootsweb.com/~engqfhs/Research/counties/lancs.htm
  Notes on Quaker records

Indexes

- Boyd's Marriage Index: Parishes and Periods of Records: Lancashire
  www.britishorigins.com/help/popup-aboutbo-bmi-parish.htm
  Click on 'Lancashire'

- IGI Batch Numbers for Lancashire (A-K), England
  freepages.genealogy.rootsweb.com/~hughwallis/IGIBatchNumbers/CountyLancashire_(A-K).htm
  Continued at **/CountyLancashire_(L-O).htm** and **/CountyLancashire_(P-Z).htm**

- Lancashire, England, Parish and Probate Records
  www.ancestry.com/search/db.aspx?dbid=5895
  Index to published registers

Publications

- The Lancashire Parish Register Society
  www.genuki.org.uk/big/eng/LAN/lprs/
  Includes list of printed registers

- Lancashire Parish Register Society
  www.mlfhs.org.uk/Bookshop/index.html
  List of registers currently available from the bookshop of the Manchester & Lancashire Family History Society

- Lancashire Family History and Heraldry Society: Current Microfiche Sales
  www.lancashire-fhhs.org.uk/shop/fiche/index.htm
  Includes many parish registers

- Liverpool & S.W. Lancs F.H.S.: Online Shop
  www.liverpool-genealogy.org.uk/acatalog/index.html
  Includes many transcripts and indexes of parish registers on fiche

- Manchester & Lancashire F.H.S. Bookshop & Mail Order
  www.mlfhs.org.uk/Bookshop.index.html
  Publications include many parish registers

- [North Meols Family History Society]
  www.nmfhssouthport.co.uk/
  Click on 'publications' for details of published registers, *etc.*

Transcript Collections on the Web

- Hibernia
  freepages.genealogy.rootsweb.com/~hibernia/
  Devoted to the Irish in Liverpool. Includes a collection of transcripts and indexes; also many links

- Index to Liverpool Registers
  www.geocities.com/liverpoolregisters/
  Collection of transcripts and indexes; also many links

Accrington

- St. James Church, Accrington, Lancashire: Parish Register Transcriptions
  www.michaellonsdale.co.uk/churchkirk/index.htm
  Index to baptisms 1813-33, marriages 1813, and burials 1813-18

Barton on Irwell

- Barton Wesleyan Chapel Burials 1804-[1866]
  www.mancuniensis.info/BartonWesleyanChapel/BWCBFP.htm
  In progress

Billinge

- Lancashire: St. Aiden, Billinge, Parish Registers
  freepages.genealogy.rootsweb.com/~copestake/lanbillingepr1332.htm
  Brief extracts

Bolton

- Saint Peter Parish Churchyard, Bolton, Greater Manchester, England
  www.interment.net/data/eng/greatman/stpet_bolton/peter.htm
  Contributed entries

Bolton le Moors

- The Bolton Parish Church Burials
  homepages.rootsweb.com/~surnamru/boltonburi.html
  For 1854 only

Charlestown

See Pendleton

Edgworth

- Edgworth Congregational Churchyard, Edgworth, Bolton, Greater Manchester, England
  www.interment.net/data/eng/greatman/edgworth/edgworth.htm
  Contributed entries

Farnworth

See Prescot

Garston

See Grassendale

Gillmoss

- Index to Marriages at St. Swithins R.C. Church, Gillmoss (1764-1856) arranged by bride's surname
  www.geocities.com/liverpoolregisters/GILLMOSSBRIDES.html
  For index by grooms, see **/GILLMOSSgrooms.html**
- [St. Swithin's R.C. Church, Gillmoss, Burials (1837-1856)]
  www.geocities.com/liverpoolregisters/STSWITHINBURIALS.html

Gisburn

- St. Mary the Virgin, Gisburn: Searchable Burial Database 1720 to 2002 from records held by St. Mary's or monuments in the graveyard
  www.gisburn.org.uk/burials/index.htm

Grassendale

- Baptisms, St. Austin's RC Church, Grassendale, Garston, Liverpool, 1856-1882
  freepages.genealogy.rootsweb.com/~hibernia/ausbap.htm

Great Carlton

- Great Carlton Transcriptions
  www.wparkinson.com/Great%20Carlton.htm
  Baptisms 1813-1904; marriages 1813-37

Great Crosby

- Burials. Ss. Peter & Paul's R.C. Church, Great Crosby, near Liverpool
  freepages.genealogy.rootsweb.com/~hibernia/sspp/sspp.htm
  Index, 19th c.

Great Sankey

See Prescot

Greengate

- Greengate Unitarian Baptisms 1825-1837
  www.salfordroots.com/GreengateUnitarianChapelBaptisms1825-1837Indexed.htm

- Greengate Unitarian Meeting House Burial Register 1826-1837
  www.salfordroots.com/GreengateUnitBurs1826-1837Indexed.htm

Huyton

- Index to marriages at St. Agnes R.C. Church, Huyton, (1871-1940) arranged by bride's surname
  www.geocities.com/liverpoolregisters/stagnesmarrbride.html
  For index by grooms, see **/STAGNESMARRGROOM.html**

Ince Blundell

- Index to Marriages at Holy Family, Ince Bludell (1831-1900) arranged by bride's surname
  www.geocities.com/liverpoolregisters/INCEBLUNDELLBRIDES.html
  For index by grooms, see **/INCEBLUNDELLGROOMS.hmtl**
- Burials/Deaths at Ince Blundell R.C. Church (1836-1861)
  www.geocities.com/liverpoolregisters/INCEBLUNDELLBURIALS.html

Kirkby

- St. Chad's, Kirkby
  mysite.wanadoo-members.co.uk/stchadskirkby
  Includes selected burial records from 1681-1940, with index *etc.*

Kirkdale

- St. Mary's Church, Kirkdale, Liverpool: marriagers extracted from LDS film #1545938, covering the period from 4th October 1874 to 11th December 1883
  www.genuki.org.uk/big/eng/LAN/Liverpool/St.Mary-marr-1874-1883.txt

Knowsley

- Knowsley Cemeteries Services
  www.knowsley.gov.uk/contract/cemetery/index.html
  Includes an offline search service

Little Carlton

- Little Carlton Transcriptions
  www.wparkinson.com/Little%20Carlton.htm
  Baptisms 1813-1978; marriages 1813-37

Little Crosby

- Little Crosby Church, St Mary's
  www.sunnyfields.freeserve.co.uk/church/
  Includes baptisms 1801-56; marriages 1835-56; deaths 1812-56 and monumental inscriptions

Liverpool

See also Grassendale

- Liverpool Area R.C. Marriage Index Home Page
  freepages.genealogy.rootsweb.com/~hibernia/mar/mar.htm
  Index of 64,000 names of the 19th c.
- Liverpool Church of England Marriage Index (1800-37)
  www.geocities.com/liverpoolregisters/COPEMARRIAGEINDEX.html
  Detaisl of an offline index
- Breaking the G.R.O. Code
  www.geocities.com/liverpoolregisters/gro.html
  How to identify the church in which a Liverpool marriage took place from the civil registration indexes (and thus identify the relevant church registers)
- Records of Catholic Churches in Liverpool
  www.genuki.org.uk/big/eng/LAN/Liverpool/cathchur.txt
  List of the holdings of Liverpool Record Office
- Liverpool Area R.C. Cemetery Search Services
  freepages.genealogy.rootsweb.com/~hibernia/bur/rccem.htm
  Details of an offline index to burial records at Ford, Yew Tree, and Ainsdale Roman Catholic Cemeteries, 1859-1909
- Liverpool Funeral, Burial in Ireland
  www.geocities.com/liverpoolregisters/defunctorum.html
  Index
- Liverpool Jewish Genealogy Service
  www.ljgs.org/
  Includes index to registers
- Liverpool Marriages and Obituaries
  freepages.genealogy.rootsweb.com/~liverpool/main.html
  Click on title. From the *Liverpool Mercury,* 1811-34; also includes other information from Liverpool newspapers

- Allerton Cemetery, Liverpool
mysite.wanadoo-members.co.uk/allertoncemetery
Contributed entries from burial registers and monumental inscriptions
- Baptisms at All Saints C. of E. Church, Liverpool (1835-1838)
www.geocities.com/liverpoolregisters/ALLSAINTSBAPTISMSa-z.html
- Burials at All Saints C. of E. Church, Liverpool (1835-1838)
www.geocities.com/liverpoolregisters/ALLSAINTSBURIALSa__z.html
- Liverpool Cemeteries
freepages.genealogy.rootsweb.com/~liverpoolcem/
Index to Anfield Cemetery
- Baptisms at Holy Trinity C. of E. Church, Liverpool (1802-1812)
www.geocities.com/liverpoolregisters/holytrinitybaptisms.html
- Burials at Holy Trinity C. of E. Church, Liverpool, (1802-1812)
www.geocities.com/liverpoolregisters/holytrinityburials.html
Index
- Burials at St. Andrew C. of E. Church, Liverpool (1816-1854)
www.geocities.com/liverpoolregisters/standrewburials.html
- Burials at St. Anne R.C. Church, Overbury St., Liverpool
www.geocities.com/liverpoolregisters/STANNEBURIALS.htm
- Baptisms at St. Anthony's R.C. Church, Liverpool
freepages.genealogy.rootsweb.com/~hibernia/baptisms/antbap.htm
Contributed entries
- Index of Marriages at St. Anthony's R.C. Church, Liverpool, L3, 1865-1906
freepages.genealogy.rootsweb.com/~hibernia/mar/ant3mar.htm
- Burials at St. Anthony's R.C. Church, Liverpool, 1847
freepages.genealogy.rootsweb.com/~hibernia/bur/ant/ant47.htm
Index
- Index to the Marriages at St. Francis Xavier R.C. Church, Liverpool, 1856-63
freepages.genealogy.rootsweb.com/~hibernia/mar/sfx2.htm
- Index of Baptisms, St. George's Presbyterian Church, Liverpool, 1856-1905
freepages.genealogy.rootsweb.com/~hibernia/baptisms/geobap.htm
- St. James Cemetery, Liverpool
www.g0ifk.u-net.com/
Includes database
- Burials at St. Martin in the Fields C. of E. Church, Liverpool (1829-1865)
www.geocities.com/liverpoolregisters/STMARTININTHEFIELDSBURIALS.html
- Burials at St. Nicholas R.C. Church, Liverpool, 1813-54
freepages.genealogy.rootsweb.com/~hibernia/bur/nic/nic.htm
- Liverpool St. Peter's Marriages
www.familyhistoryonline.co.uk/database/SWLancsFHSmar.shtml
Pay per view index, 1860-1837
- Burials at St. Philip C. of E. Church, Liverpool (1816-1876)
www.geocities.com/liverpoolregisters/STPHILIPBURIALS.html
- Some Marriages at St. Sylveter's R.C. Church, Liverpool, L5
freepages.genealogy.rootsweb.com/~hibernia/mar/sylmar.htm
Contributed entries

Lydiate

- Index to Marriages at Our Lady R.C. Church, Lydiate (1791-1900) arranged by bride's surname
www.geocities.com/liverpoolregisters/LYDIATEBRIDES.html
For index by grooms, see **/LYDIATEGROOMS.html**

Manchester

- Manchester Church History
  www.genuki.org.uk/big/eng/LAN/Manchester/church_history.html
  Includes brief notes on registers, and on 'the reasons for marriage in the Cathedral'.

New Windsor

See Salford

Oldham

- Registers of Oldham Church, 1558-1661
  www.newenglandancestors.org/research/database/oldham/default.asp

Pendleton

- Brunswick Chapel Baptisms 1814-1837
  www.salfordroots.com/Brunswickchapelbaptisms1814-1837.htm
- Salford, Pendleton Methodist New Connexion, Baptisms, 1813-1837
  www.salfordroots.com/MethNewConnexion1813-1837Indexedbaptisms.htm
- Baptisms at the Independent Chapel, Charlestown, Pendleton 1836-1837
  www.salfordroots.com/CharlestownIndBaptisms1836-1837.htm

Prescot

- Prescot Church
  prescotchurch.merseyworld.com
  Click on 'Timelines' and 'Records' for details of parish and chapelry registers for Prescot, Farnworth, Rainford Chapel, St. Helen's and Great Sankey

Prestwich

- Marriages for Prestwich, Lancashire (1754-1800)
  www.familyhistoryonline.co.uk/database/ManLancsFHSmars.shtml
  Pay per view

Rainford Chapel

See Prescot

St. Helen's

See Prescot

Salford

- Salford Parish Transcriptions
  www.salfordroots.com/page8.htm
  Collection of transcripts, separately listed here
- Chapel St. Independent Baptisms 1820-1834
  www.salfordroots.com/Chapelstindbaptismxtra.htm
  Index
- Salford, Christ Church, King Street, Bible Christians: Baptisms in Burial Register
  www.salfordroots.com/BaptismsinBurialRegisterChristChKSBCA-B.htm
  Continued on 4 further pages
- Salford, Christ Church, King Street Bible Christians Burials 1800
  www.salfordroots.com/1800ChristChKSBCBurialsIndexed.htm
  Continued to 1813 on 46 further pages
- Salford New Windsor Baptisms 1800-1837
  www.salfordroots.com/SalfordNewWindsorBaptisms1800-1837INDEXED.htm
  Index
- Salford New Windsor Burials 1800-1837
  www.salfordroots.com/NewWindsorBurials1800-1837INDEXED.htm

Toxteth Park

- Toxteth Park Cemetery
  freepages.genealogy.rootsweb.com/~toxtethparkcemetery/
  Includes general information on registers

Warrington

- Tracing a Grave
  www.warrington.gov.uk/services/bereavement/tracing.htm
  In Warrington; a database is forthcoming

Woolton

- Index to the Marriages at St. Mary's R.C. Church, Woolton, Liverpool, 1756 to 1907
  freepages.genealogy.rootsweb.com/~hibernia/mar/mary/mary.htm

Leicestershire

Civil Registration

- Registration Districts in Leicestershire
  www.fhsc.org.uk/genuki/REG/lei.htm
  Between 1837 and 1930
- [St. Catherine's House Marriage Index, Jan-March, 1849. District 15. Leicestershire/Nottinghamshire
  www.cs.ncl.ac.uk/genuki/StCathsTranscriptions/CATH4915.TXT

Parish & Non-Parochial Registers: Introductory Pages & Lists

- Census and parish registers
  www.leics.gov.uk/index/community/libraries/library_services/census.htm
  Includes list of parish registers held in Leicestershire libraries
- Leicestershire
  www.sog.org.uk/prc/leicester.html
  Parish registers, printed, typescript, etc., in the library of the Society of Genealogists
- Quaker Family History Society: Leicestershire & Rutland
  www.rootsweb.com/~engqfhs/Research/counties/leics.htm
  Notes on Quaker records

Indexes

- Marriage Database
  www.uk-genealogy.org.uk/datafiles/marriagesearch.html
  Index to various registers, especially in Leicestershire and the East Midlands
- Leicestershire and Rutland Stray Marriages
  www.familyhistoryonline.co.uk/database/LEIStrayMarriages.shtml
  Pay per view index
- Leicestershire and Rutland Burial Index
  www.familyhistoryonline.co.uk/database/LEIBurialIndex.shtml
  Pay per view
- Free Reg: Leicestershire
  freereg.rootsweb.com/parishes/lei/index.htm
  Details of the registers currently included in a project to index births, deaths and marriages
- IGI Batch Numbers for Leicester, England
  freepages.genealogy.rootsweb.com/~hughwallis/IGIBatchNumbers/CountyLeicester.htm
- Leicestershire, England: Parish and Probate Records
  www.ancestry.com/search/db.aspx?dbid=5897
  Index to published registers

Publications

- Leicestershire & Rutland Family History Society: Society Publications
  lrfhs.org.uk/publications.html
  Includes parish registers, *etc.*
- The Leicestershire Parish Register
  www.leicesterproject.com/
  Details of a CD

Transcript Collections on the Web

- Transcripts of Parish Records
  freespace.virgin.net/guy.etchells/Parish.htm
  Collection of transcripts

Appleby

- Village Families: Inhabitants of Appleby, 1560-1701
  www.applebymagna.org.uk/appleby_history/villagers_early_modern_inhabitants.htm
  Lists of surnames from the parish register, probate records, etc.

Asfordby

- Asfordby Parish Records
  freepages.genealogy.rootsweb.com/~framland/fp/Asfindex.htm
  Marriages 1564-1837

Bottesford

- Bottesford Parish Records
  freespace.virgin.net/guy.etchells/Botprindex.htm
  Baptisms 1729-1816; marriages 1563-1812; burials 1730-1900

- Strays: Bottesford People appearing in surrounding registers
  freepages.genealogy.rootsweb.com/~framland/strays.htm

Desford
- Desford
  www.uk-genealogy.org.uk/
  Search 'Desford'. Marriages 1559-1837

Eastwell
- Eastwell Parish Records
  freespace.virgin.net/guy.etchells/Eastprindex.htm
  Marriages 1588-1749 and 1754-1832

Goadby Marwood
- Goadby Marwood Parish Records
  freepages.genealogy.rootsweb.com/~framland/fp/Goadindex.htm
  Marriages 1657-1837

Hinckley
- Hinckley General Baptist Births
  freepages.genealogy.rootsweb.com/~blanchec/hinckbirth.htm
  Mainly for the 1820's and 1830's

Hoton
- Hoton Parish Records: Marriages 1654 to 1826
  freespace.virgin.net/guy.etchells/Hoton.htm
  Transcription

Leicester
- St. Margaret's Marriage Index
  www.geocities.com/Heartland/Pond/1598/stmargs.html
  Index to a Leicester church register, 1837-97

Long Clawson
- Long Clawson Parish Records
  freespace.virgin.net/guy.etchells/LCprindex.htm
  Marriages 1558-1921; burials 1748-1769. In progress

Lutterworth
- Leicestershire Records
  www.genogold.com/leicestershire_search.php
  Searchable database of Lutterworth records (presumably registers)

Muston
- Muston Parish Records
  freespace.virgin.net/guy.etchells/MUprindex.htm
  Marriages 1562-1812

Netherseal
- Netherseal & Overseal Parish Pages
  freepages.genealogy.rootsweb.com/~brett/seal/seal.htm
  Includes list of registers, transcripts, films *etc.,* also Netherseal baptisms, marriages & burials 1725-1812; Overseal baptisms & burials 1842-71

Overseal
See Netherseal

Packington
- Packington General Baptist Births 1761-1767
  freepages.genealogy.rootsweb.com/~blanchec/packbirth.htm

Peckleton
- Peckleton
  www.uk-genealogy.org.uk/
  Search 'Peckleton'. Marriages. 1567-1763

Quorndon
- Quorndon Parish Records
  freespace.virgin.net/guy.etchells/Quprindex.htm
  Marriages 1576-1837

Ratcliffe Culey
- Ratcliffe Culey
  www.mdlp.co.uk/resources/ratcliffe/index.htm
  Includes index to marriages 1752-1925, and burials 1710-1969

Sheepy Magna
- Sheepy Magna
  www.mdlp.co.uk/resources/Sheepy/
  Click on 'Burials'. Includes index, 1710-1995, with related monumental inscriptions

Sibson

- Sibson
  www.mdlp.co.uk/resources/Sibson/index.htm
  Burials from the parish register; forthcoming

Thringstone

- St. Andrews, Thringstone: from the parish registers
  www.geocities.com/oliveshark53/StAndreg.htm

Wartnaby

- Wartnaby Parish Records Marriages 1635 to 1838
  freespace.virgin.net/guy.etchells/Wart.htm

Lincolnshire

Civil Registration

- Lincolnshire District Registrars
  www.genealogy-links.co.uk/html/lin.dist.reg.html
- Registration Districts in Lincolnshire
  www.fhsc.org.uk/genuki/REG/lin.htm
  Between 1837 and 1930
- Civil Registration
  www.genuki.org.uk/big/eng/LIN/civilreg.html
  www.rootsweb.com/englin/civilreg.htm
  On the Lincolnshire Genuki and Genweb pages, but of general as well as Lincolnshire interest
- Registration Service
  www.lincolnshire.gov.uk/index.asp?CatId=2944
  Includes page on 'Tracing your family tree'.

Parish & Non-Parochial Registers: Introductory Pages & Lists

- Lincolnshire Church and Parish Records
  www.genuki.org.uk/big/eng/LIN/churchrecs.html
  www.rootsweb.com/~englin/churchrecs.htm
  Introductory page from Genuki and Genweb
- Parish Registers and Bishops' Transcripts deposited at Lincolnshire Archives
  www.lincolnshire.gov.uk/section.asp?docId=27637
- Lincolnshire Non-Conformist Records
  www.genuki.org.uk/big/eng/LIN/nonconformist.html
  Introductory page from Genuki
- Records of Non-conformist Denominations
  www.lincolnshire.gov.uk/section.asp?docId=28147
  At Lincolnshire Archives
- Lincolnshire
  www.sog.org.uk/prc/lincolnshire.html
  Parish registers, printed, typescripts, etc., in the library of the Society of Genealogists

- Quaker Family History Society: Lincolnshire
  www.rootsweb.com/~engqfhs/Research/counties/lincs.htm
  Notes on Quaker records

Indexes

- Parish Registers
  www.srichards.freeserve.co.uk/genealo-parishregisters.htm
  Index of Lincolnshire baptisms, marriages and burials for selected parishes and names

- National Burial Index (Lincolnshire F.H.S.)
  www.familyhistoryonline.co.uk/database/NBILincolnshireFHS.shtml
  Pay per view

- National Burial Index (Isle of Axholme F.H.S.)
  www.familyhistoryonline.co.uk/database/NBIIsleofAxholmeFHS.shtml

- Lincolnshire Workhouse Deaths
  www.familyhistoryonline.co.uk/databaseLincsFHSWorkDeath.shtml
  Pay per view

- Lincolnshire Cemetery Registers
  www.familyhistoryonline.co.uk/database/LincsFHSCemReg.shtml
  Pay per view

- IGI Batch Numbers for Lincoln, England
  freepages.genealogy.rootsweb.com/~hughwallis/BatchNumbers/CountyLincoln_(A-J).htm
  Continued at **/CountyLincoln_(K-R).htm** and **/CountyLincoln_(S-Z).htm**

- Lincolnshire, England: Parish and Probate Records
  www.ancestry.com/search/db.aspx?dbid=5900
  Index to published registers

Marriage Licence Allegations

- Lincolnshire Marriage Bonds and Allegations
  www.familyhistoryonline.co.uk/database/LincolnshireFHSmlb.shtml
  Pay per view. Covers the Diocese of Lincoln, but predominantly Lincolnshire

Publications

- Lincolnshire Family History Society: Publications List
  www.genuki.org.uk/big/eng/LIN/lfhs/Documents/PublicationsList.pdf
  Many indexes to marriage and burial registers on fiche, *etc.*

- The Isle of Axholme Family History Society Publications List
  www.keithanderson.co.uk/axholme/order.htm
  Includes many parish registers

- The Isle of Axholme: Marriage Index Database Programme
  www.keithanderson.co.uk/axholme/advert.htm
  Details of a database for sale on floppy disks

Barton on Humber

- Barton Parish Register
  www.stpetersbarton.org.uk/parish.php
  Searchable database

Bassingham

- Bassingham Parish Register
  www.genuki.org.uk/big/eng/LIN/Bassingham/bassingham_register.txt
  Marriages 1838-50; burials 1843-57, *etc.*

Belton

- Belton Parish Register Extracts
  freepages.genealogy.rootsweb.com/~maureenbryson/id/111.htm
  Selected surnames only

Boston

- Register of the Anglican Church, St. Botolph, at Boston
  www.genuki.org.uk/big/eng/LIN/Boston/boston_register.txt
  Brief extracts only of baptisms 1785-1832, burials 1806-14, *etc.*

Brigg

- Brigg Baptisms
  www.genuki.org.uk/big/eng/LIN/Brigg/brigg_register.txt
  Brief extracts for 1885-6

Burton Pedwardine

- Parish Registers: Burton Pedwardine
  freepages.genealogy.rootsweb.com/~heckington/Nearby_Villages/Burton_Pedwardine/burton_pedwardine.html
  Click on 'Parish Registers'. Baptisms 1561-1854; marriages 1561-1888; burials 1561-1855

Closterworth

- Register (partial extract) of the Anglican Church at Colsterworth
  www.genuki.org.uk/big/eng/LIN/Colsterworth/colsterworth_register.txt
  Extracts of marriages, 1873-1925, & burials, 1813-1915

Crowle

- Crowle Parish Register Extracts
  freepages.genealogy.rootsweb.com/~maureenbryson/id54.htm
  Selected surnames only

Denton

- Denton, Lincoln, Parish Register Extract
  www.genuki.org.uk/big/eng/LIN/Denton/denton_register.txt
  Brief extracts

Doddington Pigot

- [Doddington Pigot Marriages 1562-1812]
  www.uk-genealogy.org.uk/datafiles/marriagesearch.html
  Search 'Doddington Pigot'.

Epworth

- Epworth Parish Register Extracts
  freepages.genealogy.rootsweb.com/~maureenbryson/id110.htm
  Selected surnames only

Fleet

- Fleet Lincoln Parish Register Extract
  www.genuki.org.uk/big/eng/LIN/Fleet/fleet_register.txt
  Brief

Frodingham

- Frodingham Search
  www.genogold.com/frodingham/frodingham_search.php
  Parish register database
- Parish Register Extracts
  www.genuki.org.uk/big/eng/LIN/Frodingham/frodingham_register.txt
  For Frodingham, 1674-5. Brief

Gosberton

- Gosberton Parish Register
  www.genuki.org.uk/big/eng/LIN/Gosberton/gosberton_par_reg.txt
  Extracts, 1657-1857

Great Carlton

- Great Carlton Transcriptions
  www.wparkinson.com/Great%20Carlton.htm
  Baptisms, 1813-1904; marriages 1813-37

Grimsby

- Grimsby Hebrew Congregation Marriages
  www.jewishgen.org/jcr-uk/Community/Gr/marriage.htm

Haxey

- Haxey Parish Register Extracts
  freepages.genealogy.rootsweb.com/~maureenbryson/id112.htm
  Selected surnames only

Heckington

- Parish Registers Heckington
  freepages.genealogy.rootsweb.com/~heckington/Church_Records/church_records.html
  Click on 'Records' and 'Parish Registers'. Index
- Heckington Burials 1561-1649
  www.genuki.org.uk/big/eng/LIN/Heckington/heckington_burials_1561.pdf

Holbeach

- Holbeach Parish Registers
  www.pcug.org.au/~bthompso/holbeach/readme.htm
  Scanned transcript of a register originally published 1892.

Langton by Partney

- Langton by Partney Burials commencing 1761
  www.genuki.org.uk/big/eng/LIN/LangtonPartney/langtonpartney_register.txt
  To 1812

Little Carlton

- Little Carlton Transcriptions
  www.wparkinson.com/Little%20Carlton.htm
  Baptisms 1813-1978; marriages 1813-1837

Long Bennington

- Anglican Church Register Extract, Long Bennington, Lincolnshire
  www.genuki.org.uk/big/eng/LIN/LongBennington/longbennington_register.txt
  Baptisms 1623-1812; marriages 1632-1919; burials 1666-1900. Incomplete

North Hykeham

- North Hykeham Parish Registers
  www.wparkinson.com/Hykeham/nhpage.htm
  Various 18-19th c. transcripts and indexes

Pinchbeck

- Pinchbeck, Lincolnshire, Burials away from Home
  www.genuki.org.uk/big/eng/LIN/Pinchbeck/pinchbeck_awayburial.txt
  1700-1724/5

Quadring

- Quadring Baptisms (partial extract)
  www.genuki.org.uk/big/eng/LIN/Quadring/quadring_register.txt
  1825-53

Sandtoft

- Sandtoft
  privatewww.essex.ac.uk/~alanfamily/G-Sandtoft.html
  Includes Huguenot marriages 1643-71, baptisms 1642-85, & burials 1650-51.

South Hykeham

- South Hykeham Parish Registers
  www.wparkinson.com/Hykeham/shpage.htm
  Various transcripts and indexes, 19-20th c.

Spalding

- Parish Register Extract of Spalding, Lincolnshire
  www.genuki.org.uk/big/eng/LIN/Spalding/spalding_reg.txt
  Brief extracts only, 1659-1885

Sutton St. Edmund

- Sutton St. Edmund Marriages: Index of Marriages found in the Parish Registers for Sutton St. Edmund, Lincolnshire from 1706-1892
  contueor.com/wisbech/indexes/sutton_st_edmund.htm

Tetney

- Tetney Transcriptions
  www.wparkinson.com/Tetney.htm
  Baptisms 1813-49; Marriages 1813-37.

Norfolk

Civil Registration

- Civil Registration
  www.origins.org.uk/genuki/NFK/Norfolk/civil_reg/

- Registration Districts in Norfolk
  www.fhsc.org.uk/genuki/REG/nfk.htm
  Between 1837 and 1930

- Register Offices in Norfolk
  www.norfolk.gov.uk/communities/register/register_offices.asp
  Notes on each office

- [St.Catherine's House Marriage Index, Jan-March, 1849. District 13. Norfolk/North Suffolk
  www.cs.ncl.ac.uk/genuki/StCathsTranscriptions/CATH4913.TXT

Parish & Non-Parochial Registers: Introductory Pages & Lists

- Norfolk Church Records
  www.origins.org.uk/genuki/NFK/norfolk/church/
  Genuki introduction

- Norfolk Record Office Parish Registers and Transcripts
  www.norfolk.gov.uk/leisure/archives/pratlist/nropratintro.htm

- Norfolk Parish Register Project
  www.cshales.freeserve.co.uk
  Includes list of transcripts held by Norfolk Family History Society

- Norfolk Family History Society Parish Register Transcripts at Kirby Hall
  www.norfolkfhs.org.uk/church/parishbmd1.html

- Norfolk
  www.sog.org.uk/prc/norfolk.html
  Parish registers, printed, typescripts, *etc.,* in the library of the Society of Genealogists

- Quaker Family History Society: Norfolk
  www.rootsweb.com/~engqfhs/Research/counties/norfolk.htm
  Notes on Quaker records

- Brides in Norfolk, England
  www.rootsweb.com/~engnfk/nrfmrsb1.html
  List of entries from submitters

- Grooms in Norfolk, England
  www.rootsweb.com/~engnfk/nrfmrsg1.html
  List of entries from submitters

Indexes

- Mid-Norfolk Baptisms
  www.familyhistoryonline.co.uk/database/MNFHSbaps.shtml
  Pay per view index

- Boyd's Marriage Index: Parishes and Period of Records: Norfolk
  www.britishorigins.com/help/popup-aboutbo-bmi-countydetails.htm
  Click on 'Norfolk'

- National Burial Index (Norfolk F.H.S.- South)
  www.familyhistoryonline.co.uk/database/NBINorfolkFHS.shtml

- National Burial Index (Mid-Norfolk F.H.S.)
  www.familyhistoryonline.co.uk/database/NBIMidNorfolkFHS.shtml
  Pay per view

- Mid-Norfolk F.H.S. National Burial Index Project
  www.mnfhs.freeuk.com/nbi.html

- Norfolk, England: Parish and Probate Records
  www.ancestry.com/search/db.aspx?dbid=5914
  Index to published registers

- IGI Batch Numbers for Norfolk, England
  freepages.genealogy.rootsweb.com/~hughwallis/IGIBatchNumbers/CountyNorfolk.htm

Newspaper Indexes

- Extracts from *Lynn Advertiser's* Marriages and Deaths 1881-1900
  ourworld.compuserve.com/homepages/Martin_Edwards_2/lynnadv.html

Transcript Collections on the Web

- Norfolk Transcription Archives
  www.genealogy.doun.org/transcriptions/
  Collection of transcripts, listed separately below

- Wisbech and the Fenlands: Indexes
  www.contueor.com/wisbech/indexes/index.htm
  Collection of indexes to parish registers, primarily from Norfolk (although Wisbech is in Cambridgeshire)

Publications
See also Suffolk

- Norfolk Family History Society Publications List and Order Form
  www.norfolkfhs.org.uk/sales/
  Includes parish and non-conformist registers

- Mid-Norfolk F.H.S. Publications List
  www.mnfhs.freeuk.com/pub.html
  Includes parish register transcriptions, burial indexes, *etc.*

- Norfolk: Church Records: Phillimore's Marriage Registers
  www.origins.org.uk/genuki/NFK/norfolk/church/phillimore.shtml
  List of parishes covered by Phillimore's series

Ashmanhaugh
- Norfolk: Tunstead & Happing District: Ashmanhaugh
  www.genealogy.doun.org/transcriptions
  Click on 'Parishes', 'A' & 'Ashmanhaugh'. Includes baptisms 1561-1812, marriages 1562-1901, & burials 1563-1811. Some years missing

Ashwellthorpe
- Norfolk: Depwade District: Ashwellthorpe
  www.genealgy.doun.org/transcriptions/
  Click on 'Parishes', 'A' & 'Ashwellthorpe. Includes bishops' transcripts 1725-1812 (incomplete)

Ashwicken
- Ashwicken-Leziate Marriages: Index of marriages found in the Archdeacon's Transcripts for Ashwicken-Leziate, Norfolk from 1729-1779
  contueor.com/wisbech/indexes/ashwicken_leziate.htm

Aslacton
- Norfolk: Depwade District: Aslacton
  www.genealogy.doun.org/transcriptions/
  Click on 'Parishes', 'A' & 'Aslacton'. Includes bishops' transcripts, 1725-1812 (incomplete)

Attleborough
- Norfolk: Wayland District: Attleborough
  www.genealogy.doun.org/transcriptions/
  Click on 'Parishes', 'A' & 'Attleborough'. Includes baptisms, 1750-72

Aylsham
- Norfolk: Aylsham District: Aylsham
  www.genealogy.doun.org/transcriptions/
  Click on 'Parishes', 'A' & 'Aylsham'. Includes baptisms 1710-1901, banns 1865-1901, marriages 1653-1901, & burials 1710-1901, *etc.*

Baconsthorpe
- Norfolk: Erpingham District: Baconsthorpe
  www.genealogy.doun.org/transcriptions/
  Click on 'Parishes', 'B' & 'Baconsthorpe'. Includes baptisms, 1755-1870, marriages, 1800-1817 and burials, 1800-1812

Barford
- Norfolk: Forehoe District: Barford
  www.genealogy.doun.org/transcriptions/
  Click on 'Parishes', 'B' & 'Barford'. Includes bishops' transcripts, 1725-1812 (some years missing)

Barnham Broom
- Norfolk: Forehoe District: Barnham Broom
  www.genealogy.doun.org/transcriptions/
  Click on 'Parishes', 'B' & 'Barnham Broom'. Includes bishops' transcripts 1725-1811 (some years missing)

Barton Turf
- Norfolk: Tunstead & Happing District: Barton Turf
  www.genealogy.doun.org/transcriptions/
  Click on 'Parishes', 'B', & 'Barton Turf'. Includes baptisms 1828-1903, banns 1840-1900, marriages 1841-1900, & burials 1840-1900. Incomplete

- Norfolk: Barton Turf: Barton Turf Parish Registers: Surnames of People who come from other Parishes
  www.origins.org.uk/genuki/NFK/places/b/barton_turf/pr_strays.shtml

Bawburgh

- Norfolk: Forehoe District: Bawburgh
  www.genealogy.doun.org/transcriptions/
  Click on 'Parishes', 'B' & 'Bawburgh'. Includes bishops' transcripts, 1725-1812 (some years missing)

Bawsey

- Bawsey Marriages: Index of Marriages found in the Archdeacons' Transcripts for Bawsey, Norfolk from 1668-1771
  contueor.com/wisbech/indexes/bawsey.htm

Beeston St. Lawrence

- Norfolk: Tunstead & Happing District: Beeston St. Lawrence
  www.genealogy.doun.org/transcriptions/
  Click on 'Parishes', 'B' & 'Beeston St. Lawrence'. Includes baptisms, 1743-1889, banns 1757-1899, marriages 1700-1837, & burials 1702-1900. Many years missing

Belaugh

- Norfolk: Aylsham District: Belaugh
  www.genealogy.doun.org/transcriptions/
  Click on 'Parishes', 'B' & 'Belaugh'. Includes baptisms, 1742-1812, banns 1757-1891 & burials 1741-1812

Besthorpe

- Norfolk: Wayland District: Besthorpe
  www.genealogy.doun.org/transcriptions/
  Click on 'Parishes', 'B' & 'Besthorpe'. Includes baptisms, 1764-1800, marriages 1754-1826, & burials 1760-1884. Some years missing

Binham

- Norfolk: Walsingham District: Binham
  www.genealogy.doun.org/transcriptions/
  Click on 'Parishes', 'W' & 'Walsingham'. Includes baptisms, 1805-58, banns 1755-1876, marriages 1755-1837 & burials 1782-1864; also bishops' transcripts 1766-1805. Incomplete

Blakeney

- Norfolk: Walsingham District: Blakeney
  www.genealogy.doun.org/transcriptions/
  Click on 'Parishes', 'B' & 'Blakeney'. Includes baptisms, 1696-1799, & marriages 1602-1788. Many years missing

Blickling

- Norfolk: Aylsham District: Blickling
  www.genealogy.doun.org/transcriptions/
  Click on 'Parishes', 'B' & 'Blickling'. Includes baptisms, 1559-1785

Brampton

- Norfolk: Aylsham District: Brampton
  www.genealogy.doun.org/transcriptions/
  Click on 'Parishes', 'B' & 'Brampton'. Includes bishops' transcripts 1601-1812 (some years missing); also marriages 1815-36

Brandon Parva

- Norfolk: Forehoe District: Brandon Parva
  www.genealogy.doun.org/transcriptions/
  Click on 'Parishes', 'B' & 'Brandon Parva'. Includes marriages & burials from bishops' transcripts, 1726-1811 (many years missing)

Bridgham

- Norfolk: Guiltcross District: Bridgham
  www.genealogy.doun.org/transcriptions/
  Click on 'Parishes', 'B' & 'Bridgham'. Includes marriages, 1837-1901 (some years missing)

Brunstead

- Norfolk: Tunstead & Happing District: Brunstead
  www.genealogy.doun.org/transcriptions/
  Click on 'Parishes', 'B' & 'Brunstead'. Includes marriages, 1561-1901. Incomplete

Bunwell

- Norfolk: Depwade District: Bunwell
  www.genealogy.doun.org/transcriptions/
  Click on 'Parishes', 'B' & 'Bunwell'. Includes bishops' transcripts, 1725-1811 (incomplete)

Burgh next Aylsham

- Norfolk: Aylsham District: Burgh next Aylsham
  www.genealogy.doun.org/transcriptions/
  Click on 'Parishes', 'B' & 'Burgh next Aylsham'. Includes baptisms 1813-50; also bishops' transcripts 1600-1812 (some years missing)

Burgh St. Margaret

- Norfolk: Flegg District: Burgh St. Margaret & St. Mary
  www.genealogy.doun.org/transcriptions/
  Click on 'Parishes', 'B' & 'Burgh St. Margaret & St. Mary'. Includes bishops' transcripts, 1761-1811 (incomplete)

Burgh St. Mary

See Burgh St. Margaret

Buxton

- Norfolk: Aylsham District: Buxton:
  www.genealogy.doun.org/transcriptions/
  Click on 'Parishes', 'B', & 'Buxton'. Baptisms 1718-1896, banns 1837-1900, marriages 1754-1837, & burials 1800-1872. Also bishops' transcripts, 1601-1812 (many years missing)
- Longevity and Child Mortality in Buxton
  www.genealogy.doun.org/transcriptions/articles/view_article.php?document_id=28918
  Based on the parish register

Carleton Forehoe

- Norfolk: Forehoe District: Carleton Forehoe
  www.genealogy.doun.org/transcriptions/
  Click on 'Parishes', 'C' & 'Carleton Forehoe'. Includes bishops' transcripts, 1725-1811 (incomplete)

Carleton Rode

- Norfolk: Depwade District: Carleton Rode
  www.genealogy.doun.org/transcriptions/
  Click on 'Parishes', 'C' & 'Carleton Rode'. Includes bishops' transcripts, 1725-1811 (incomplete)

Castle Rising

- Castle Rising Marriages: Index of Marriages found in the Archdeacons' Transcripts for Castle Rising, Norfolk, from 1736-1818
  contueor.com/wisbech/indexes/castle_rising.htm

Caston

- Norfolk: Wayland District: Caston
  www.genealogy.doun.org/transcriptions/
  Click on 'Parishes', 'C' & 'Caston'. Includes baptisms 1531-1720, & marriages 1539-1705. Many years missing

Cawston

- Norfolk: Aylsham District: Cawston
  www.genealogy.doun.org/transcriptions/
  Click on 'Parishes', 'C' & 'Cawston'. Includes baptisms, marriages and burials, 1712-1901; also banns 1754-1901 (many years missing)

Clenchwarton

- Clenchwarton Marriages: Index of Marriages found in the Archdeacons' Transcripts for Clenchwarton, Norfolk from 1668-1812
  contueor.com/wisbech/indexes/clenchwarton.htm

Cockthorpe

- Norfolk: Walsingham District: Cockthorpe
  www.genealogy.doun.org/transcriptions/
  Click on 'Parishes', 'C' & 'Cockthorpe'. Includes marriages 1817-1902. Many years missing

Colby

- Norfolk: Aylsham District: Colby
  www.genealogy.doun.org/transcriptions/
  Click on 'Parishes', 'C' & 'Colby'. Includes baptisms 1703-1800, marriages 1712-48, and burials 1713-49

Colney

- Norfolk: Henstead District: Colney
  www.genealogy.doun.org/transcriptions/
  Click on 'Parishes', 'C' & 'Colney'. Includes banns 1819-95, & marriages 1815-99. Many years missing

Coltishall

- Norfolk: Aylsham District: Coltishall
  www.genealogy.doun.org/transcriptions/
  Click on 'Parishes', 'C' & 'Coltishall'. Includes baptisms, 1805-1901, banns 1754-1901, marriages, 1754-1901, & burials 1725-1902; also bishops' transcripts 1600-1811 (many years missing)

Colton
- Norfolk: Forehoe District: Colton
www.genealogy.doun.org/transcriptions/
Click on 'Parishes', 'C' & 'Colton'. Includes baptisms 1725-1837, marriages 1703-1837, burials (from bishops' transcripts) 1729-1837

Corpusty
- Norfolk: Aylsham District: Corpusty
www.genealogy.doun.org/transcriptions/
Click on 'Parishes', 'C' & 'Corpusty'. Includes baptisms, 1718-1905 and burials 1725-1931; also bishops' transcripts 1729-1812 (many years missing)

Costessey
- Norfolk: Forehoe District: Costessey
www.genealogy.doun.org/transcriptions/
Click on 'Parishes', 'C' & 'Costessey'. Includes bishops' transcripts 1725-1812 (some years missing)

Coston
- Norfolk: Forehoe District: Coston
www.genealogy.doun.org/transcriptions/
Click on 'Parishes', 'C' & 'Coston'. Includes baptisms & burials, 1801-27

Cranworth
- Norfolk: Cranworth with Letton: Cranworth with Letton: List of Surnames in the Cranworth with Letton Baptism registers 1652-1855
www.origins.org.uk/genuki/NFK/places/c/cranworth/pr_bapt_names.shtml
- Norfolk: Cranworth with Letton: Cranworth with Letton Parish Registers: list of surnames of People who come from other parishes
www.origins.org.uk/genuki/NFK/places/c/cranworth/pr_strays.shtml

Crostwight
- Norfolk: Turstead & Happing District: Crostwight
www.genealogy.doun.org/transcriptions/
Click on 'Parishes', 'C' & 'Crostwight'. Includes baptisms, 1698-1812, marriages 1712-1836, & burials 1708-1812. Some years missing

Denver
- Denver Marriages: Index of Marriages found in the Archdeacons' Transcript for Denver, Norfolk from 1725-1812
contueor.com/wisbech/indexes/denver.htm

Deopham
- Norfolk: Forehoe District: Deopham
www.genealogy.doun.org/transcriptions/
Click on 'Parishes', 'D' & 'Deopham'. Includes bishops' transcripts, 1725-1811 (some years missing)

Dilham
- Norfolk: Tunstead & Happing District: Dilham
www.genealogy.doun.org/transcriptions/
Click on 'Parishes', 'D' & 'Dilham'. Includes baptisms, 1813-64, marriages 1755-1901, & burials, 1813-1920; also bishops' transcripts, 1813-1920. Incomplete

Downham Market
- Downham Market Marriages: Index of Marriages found in the Archdeacons' Transcripts for Downham Market, Norfolk, from 1725-1812
contueor.com/wisbech/indexes/downham_market.htm

Dunton cum Doughton
- Norfolk: Walsingham District: Dunton & Doughton
www.genealogy.doun.org/transcriptions/
Click on 'Parishes', 'D' & 'Dunton & Doughton'. Includes bishops' transcripts 1725-1740 & 1782-1812. Many years missing
- Norfolk: Dunton cum Doughton: Dunton cum Doughton Parish Registers: Surnames of People who come from other Parishes
www.origins.org.uk/genuki/NFK/places/d/dunton_cum_doughton/pr_strays.shtml
Covers 1785-1835

Earlham
- Norfolk: Norwich District: Norwich Earlham
www.genealogy.doun.org/transcriptions/
Click on 'Parishes' 'N', & 'Norwich Earlham'. Includes baptisms, 1621-1901, marriages 1813-1901, & burials 1639-1812. Incomplete

East Barsham

- Norfolk: East Barsham: East Barsham Parish Registers: People who come from other parishes
  www.origins.org.uk/genuki/NFK/places/b/barsham__east/pr__stray s.shtml
  Covers 1658-1835

East Dereham

- Norfolk: Mitford & Launditch District: East Dereham
  www.genealogy.doun.org/transcriptions/
  Click on 'Parishes', 'E' & 'East Dereham'. Includes bishops' transcripts 1771-1811. Some years missing

East Rudham

- Norfolk: Docking District: East Rudham
  www.genealogy.doun.org/transcriptions/
  Click on 'Parishes', 'E', and 'East Rudham'. Includes baptisms 1734-1854, marriages, 1734-1870, & burials 1735-1870; also bishops' transcript marriages 1760-96

East Ruston

- Norfolk: Tunstead & Happing District: East Ruston
  www.genealogy.doun.org/transcriptions/
  Click on 'Parishes', 'E' & 'East Ruston'. Includes baptisms, 1690-1901, banns 1824-1900, marriages 1692-1901, & burials 1692-1889. Incomplete

East Somerton

See Winterton

East Tuddenham

- Norfolk: Mitford & Launditch District: East Tuddenham
  www.genealogy.doun.org/transcriptions/
  Click on 'Parishes', 'E' & 'East Tuddenham'. Includes bishops' transcripts, 1725-1812. Incomplete

Easton

- Norfolk: Forehoe District: Easton
  www.genealogy.doun.org/transcriptions/
  Click on 'Parishes', 'E' & 'Easton'. Includes bishops' transcripts, 1725-1811 (many years missing)

Edgefield

- Norfolk: Erpingham District: Edgefield
  www.genealogy.doun.org/transcriptions/
  Click on 'Parishes', 'E' & 'Edgefield'. Includes baptisms (bishops' transcripts) 1730-67

Edingthorpe

- Norfolk: Tunstead & Happing District: Edingthorpe
  www.genealogy.doun.org/transcriptions/
  Click on 'Parishes', 'E' & 'Edingthorpe'. Includes bishops' transcripts, 1725-1812. Some years missing

Emneth

- Emneth Baptisms: Index of selected baptisms found in both the Parish Register and Bishops' Transcripts for Emneth, Norfolk from 1559-1830
  contueor.com/wisbech/indexes/emneth__bp.htm

- Emneth Baptisms Register: Extract from 1808
  freepages.genealogy.rootsweb.com/~cawthorn/Transcripts/Emneth__Baptisms__1808.html

- Emneth Marriages: Index of Marriages found in the Parish Register and Bishops' Transcripts for Emneth, Norfolk from 1599-1852
  contueor.com/wisbech/indexes/emneth.htm

Fakenham

- Norfolk: Walsingham District: Fakenham
  www.genealogy.doun.org/transcriptions/
  Click on 'Parishes', 'F' & 'Fakenham'. Includes marriages 1719-1837

Field Dalling

- Norfolk: Walsingham District: Field Dalling
  www.genealogy.doun.org/transcriptions/
  Click on 'Parishes', 'F' & 'Field Dalling'. Includes baptisms, 1812-1902

Forncett St. Mary

- Norfolk: Depwade District: Forncett St. Mary
  www.genealogy.doun.org/transcriptions/
  Click on 'Parishes', 'F' & 'Forncett St. Mary'. Includes bishops' transcripts, 1725-1808 (incomplete)

Foulden

- Norfolk: Swaffham District: Foulden
  www.genealogy.doun.org/transcriptions/
  Click on 'Parishes', 'F' & 'Foulden'. Includes baptisms, 1702-1836, banns 1755-1824, marriages 1702-1837 & burials 1703-1921

Frettenham

- Norfolk: St. Faith's District: Frettenham
  www.genealogy.doun.org/transcriptions/
  Click on 'Parishes', 'F' & 'Frettenham'. Includes baptisms 1558-1900, banns 1837-1900, marriages 1558-1836, & burials 1559-1811. Some years missing

Fritton

- Norfolk: Depwade District: Fritton
  www.genealogy.doun.org/transcriptions/
  Click on 'Parishes', 'F' & 'Fritton'. Includes baptisms 1775-1870, marriages 1754-1812, & burials 1775-1812; also bishops' transcript baptisms 1890-1902

Garveston

- Norfolk: Mitford & Launditch District: Garveston
  www.genealogy.doun.org/transcriptions/
  Click on 'Parishes, 'G' & 'Garveston'. Includes marriages 1745-1800 (many years missing)

Geldeston

- Norfolk: Tunstead & Happing District: Geldeston
  www.genealogy.doun.org/transcriptions/
  Click on 'Parishes', 'G' & 'Geldeston'. Includes banns 1817-34. Many years missing

Great Ellingham

- Norfolk: Wayland District: Great Ellingham
  www.genealogy.doun.org/transcriptions/
  Click on 'Parishes', 'G' & 'Great Ellingham'. Includes baptisms, 1815-50, marriages 1789-1837, & burials 1729-1847. Many years missing

Great Poringland

- Norfolk: Henstead District: Great Poringland
  www.genealogy.doun.org/transcriptions/
  Click on 'Parishes', 'G' & 'Great Poringland'. Includes bishops' transcripts, 1817 only

Great Snoring

- Norfolk: Walsingham District: Great Snoring
  www.genealogy.doun.org/transcriptions/
  Click on 'Parishes', 'G' & 'Great Snoring'. Includes marriages 1560-1902 (incomplete)

Great Walsingham

- Norfolk: Walsingham District: Great Walsingham
  www.genealogy.doun.org/transcriptions/
  Click on 'Parishes', 'G' & 'Great Walsingham'. Includes baptisms, 1727-1812, marriages 1727-53, & burials 1782-1812

Great Yarmouth

- Norfolk: Great Yarmouth District: Yarmouth, Great
  www.genealogy.doun.org/transcriptions/
  Click on 'Parishes', 'Y', & 'Yarmouth, Great'. Includes Wesleyan Methodist baptisms, 1795-1815 & 1820-37

- Norfolk: Great Yarmouth District: Yarmouth St. Nicholas
  www.genealogy.doun.org/transcriptions/
  Click on 'Parishes', 'Y', & 'Yarmouth St. Nicholas'. Includes baptisms 1757-1800, marriages 1756-17, & burials 1757-1800

- The Naval Hospital Burials at Yarmouth
  www.genealogy.doun.org/transcriptions/articles/view_article.php?document_id=25610
  Article partly based on the parish registers

Gresham

- Norfolk: Erpingham District: Gresham
  www.genealogy.doun.org/transcriptions/
  Click on 'Parishes', 'G' & 'Gresham'. Includes baptisms, 1813-39 & 1850-95

Hackford

- Norfolk: Forehoe District: Hackford
  www.genealogy.doun.org/transcriptions/
  Click on 'Parishes', 'H' & 'Hackford'. Includes baptisms, 1689-1794, marriages 1692-1783, & burials 1689-1794. Incomplete

Hainford

- Norfolk St. Faith's District: Hainford
  www.genealogy.doun.org/transcriptions/
  Click on 'Parishes', 'H' & 'Hainford'. Includes baptisms, marriages & burials, 1700-1902

Hapton

- Norfolk: Depwade District: Hapton
  www.genealogy.doun.org/transcriptions/
  Click on 'Parishes', 'H' & 'Hapton'. Includes bishops' transcript baptisms, 1845

Hautbois Magna

- Norfolk: Aylsham District: Hautbois Magna
  www.genealogy.doun.org/transcriptions/
  Click on 'Parishes', 'H' & 'Hautbois Magna'. Includes baptisms 1563-1699 & 1800-1812, banns (odd years 1820-1903), marriages 1563-1901, & burials 1568-1812; also bishops' transcripts 1702-1870 (many years missing)

Hevingham

- Norfolk: Aylsham District: Hevingham
  www.genealogy.doun.org/transcriptions/
  Click on 'Parishes', 'H' & 'Hevingham'. Includes baptisms, marriages, & burials, 1800-1902; also some banns 1800-1900

Heydon

- Norfolk: Aylsham District: Heydon
  www.genealogy.doun.org/transcriptions/
  Click on 'Parishes', 'H' & 'Heydon'. Includes baptisms, 1698-1911

Hickling

- Norfolk: Tunstead & Happing District: Hickling
  www.genealogy.doun.org/transcriptions/
  Click on 'Parishes', 'H' & 'Hickling'. Includes marriages 1657-1708. Incomplete

Hingham

- Norfolk: Forehoe District: Hingham
  www.genealogy.doun.org/transcriptions/
  Click on 'Parishes', 'H' & 'Hingham'. Includes baptisms 1683-1749, marriages 1701-26, & burials 1683-1726. Incomplete

Hockering

- Norfolk: Mitford & Launditch District: Hockering
  www.genealogy.doun.org/transcriptions/
  Click on 'Parishes', 'H' & 'Hockering'. Includes bishops' transcripts, 1725-1811. Incomplete

Hockwold

- Norfolk: Thetford District: Hockwold
  www.genealogy.doun.org/transcriptions/
  Click on 'Parishes', 'H' & 'Hockwold'. Includes baptisms, 1640-68, marriages 1662-8, & burials 1658-68. Incomplete

Holm Hale

- Norfolk: Swaffham District: Holm Hale
  www.genealogy.doun.org/transcriptions/
  Click on 'Parishes', 'H' & 'Holm Hale'. Includes baptisms 1758-1812, & burials 1709-1812. Incomplete

Holt

- Norfolk: Erpingham District: Holt
  www.genealogy.doun.org/transcriptions/
  Click on 'Parishes', 'H', & 'Holt'. Includes baptisms, 1738-1851, marriages 1738-75, & burials 1748-75. Some years missing

Honing

- Norfolk: Tunstead & Happing District: Honing
  www.genealogy.doun.org/transcriptions/
  Click on 'Parishes', 'H' & 'Honing'. Includes baptisms, 1630-1902, marriages 1630-1836 & burials 1630-1901. Incomplete

Honingham

- Norfolk: St. Faith's District: Honingham
  www.genealogy.doun.org/transcriptions/
  Click on 'Parishes', 'H' & 'Honingham'. Includes bishops' transcripts 1726-1812. Some years missing

Horsham St. Faith cum Newton

- Norfolk: St. Faith District: Horsham St. Faith cum Newton
  www.genealogy.doun.org/transcriptions/
  Click on 'Parishes', 'H' & 'Horsham St. Faith cum Newton'. Includes baptisms, 1695-1707; also bishops' transcripts, 1670-1811 (many years missing)

Horstead cum Staninghall

- Norfolk: St. Faith's District: Horstead cum Staninghall
  www.genealogy.doun.org/transcriptions/
  Click on 'Parishes', 'H' & 'Horstead cum Staninghall'. Includes baptisms 1812-1900, & burials 1812-1910; also bishops' transcripts 1601-1811. Many years missing

Hoveton St. John

- Norfolk: Tunstead & Happing District: Hoveton St. John
  www.genealogy.doun.org/transcriptions/
  Click on 'Parishes', 'H', & 'Hoveton St. John'. Includes baptisms 1673-1899, banns 1754-95, marriages 1674-1699 & 1800-1899, & burials 1673-1733 & 1800-1899. Many years missing

Hoveton St. Peter

- Norfolk: Tunstead & Happing District: Hoveton St. Peter
  www.genealogy.doun.org/transcriptions/
  Click on 'Parishes', 'H' & 'Hoveton St. Peter'. Includes baptisms 1700-1899, banns 1823, marriages 1700-1897, & burials 1701-1899. Many years missing

Hunworth

- Norfolk: Erpingham District: Hunworth
  www.genealogy.doun.org/transcriptions/
  Click on 'Parishes', 'H' & 'Hunworth'. Includes baptisms 1760-1812, & burials 1757-1813

Ingham

- Norfolk: Tunstead & Happing District: Ingham
  www.genealogy.doun.org/transcriptions/
  Click on 'Parishes', 'I' & 'Ingham'. Includes baptisms 1698-1901, & marriages 1700-1799. Some years missing

Islington

See Tilney

Irstead

- Norfolk: Tunstead & Happing District: Irstead
  www.genealogy.doun.org/transcriptions/
  Click on 'Parishes', 'I' & 'Irstead'. Includes baptisms, marriages & burials, 1700-1902. Incomplete

Ketteringham

- Norfolk: Henstead District: Ketteringham: Register
  www.genealogy.doun.org/transcriptions/
  Click on 'Parishes', 'K', & 'Ketteringham'. Includes baptisms, marriages & burials, 1800-1905 (some years missing)

Kettlestone

- Norfolk: Walingham District: Kettlestone
  www.genealogy.doun.org/transcriptions/
  Click on 'Parishes', 'K' & 'Kettlestone'. Includes baptisms, 1733-1903, marriages 1734-1800 & burials 1733-1800. Incomplete

King's Lynn

- Lynn St. Margaret Marriages: index of Marriages found in the Archdeacons' Transcripts for Lynn St. Margaret, Norfolk from 1667-1670, 1675-1677 & 1706-1710
  contueor.com/wisbech/indexes/lynn_st_margaret.htm

Lammas with Little Hautbois

- Norfolk: Aylsham District: Lammas with Little Hautbois
  www.genealogy.doun.org/transcriptions/
  Click on 'Parishes', 'L' & 'Lammas with Little Hautbois'. Includes baptisms 1771-1881, & burials 1777-1812

Langham

- Norfolk: Walsingham District: Langham
  www.genealogy.doun.org/transcriptions/
  Click on 'Parishes', 'L' & 'Langham'. Includes baptisms, 1801-80, marriages 1755-1812, & burials 1801-12

Lessingham

- Norfolk: Tunstead & Happing District: Lessingham
  www.genealogy.doun.org/transcriptions/
  Click on 'Parishes', 'L' & 'Lessingham'. Includes marriages 1754-1837, & burials 1783-1811. Incomplete

Letton

See Cranworth

Little Snoring

- Norfolk: Walsingham District: Little Snoring
  www.genealogy.doun.org/transcriptions/
  Click on 'Parishes', 'L' & 'Little Snoring'. Includes baptisms, 1738-1816

Loddon

- Norfolk: Mutford District: Loddon
  www.genealogy.doun.org/transcriptions/
  Click on 'Documents', 'Mutford', & 'Loddon'. Includes baptisms, 1813-1901
- Norfolk: Loddon & Clavering District: Loddon
  www.genealogy.doun.org/transcriptions/
  Click on 'Parishes', 'L' & 'Loddon'. Includes banns 1880-1901, marriages 1813-1901, & burials 1813-51

Martham

- Norfolk: Flegg District: Martham
  www.genealogy.doun.org/transcriptions/
  Click on 'Parishes, 'M' & 'Martham'. Includes baptisms, 1558-1692, marriages 1587-1692 & burials 1558-1691; also baptisms & burials from bishops' transcripts 1840-53 (incomplete)

Mattishall

- Norfolk: Mitford & Launditch District: Mattishall
  www.genealogy.doun.org/transcriptions/
  Click on 'Parishes', 'M' & 'Mattishall'. Includes bishops' transcripts, 1726-1812 (some years missing)

Mintlyn

- Mintlyn Marriages: index of Marriages found in the Archdeacons' Transcripts for Mintlyn, Norfolk from 1670-1771
  contueor.com/wisbech/indexes/mintlyn.htm

Morley St. Peter

- Norfolk: Forehoe District: Morley St. Peter
  www.genealogy.doun.org/transcriptions/
  Click on 'Parishes', 'M' & 'Morley St. Peter'. Includes baptisms 1732-1812, marriages 1729-45, & burials 1727-1812. Incomplete

Morningthorpe

- Norfolk: Depwade District: Morningthorpe:
  www.genealogy.doun.org/transcriptions/
  Click on 'Parishes', 'M', & 'Morningthorpe'. Includes a few banns 1755-82, marriages 1754-1811 (incomplete); also bishops' transcripts 1614-1738 (many years missing)

Morston

- Norfolk: Walsingham District: Morston
  www.genealogy.doun.org/transcriptions/
  Click on 'Parishes', 'M' & 'Morston'. Includes baptisms, 1837-42, banns 1754-1812, & marriages 1754-1837. Incomplete

Neatishead

- Norfolk: Tunstead & Happing District: Neatishead
  www.genealogy.doun.org/transcriptions/
  Click on 'Parishes', 'N' & 'Neatishead'. Includes baptisms 1700-1901, banns 1837-1901, marriages 1740-1837, & burials 1740-1900. Incomplete

Necton

- Norfolk: Swaffham District: Necton
  www.genealogy.doun.org/transcriptions/
  Click on 'Parishes', 'N' & 'Necton'. Includes marriages 1722-36

Needham

- Norfolk: Depwade District: Needham
  www.genealogy.doun.org/transcriptions/
  Click on 'Parishes', 'N', & 'Needham'. Includes baptisms, marriages & burials, 1794-1811; also a few bishops' transcripts

North Barsham

- Norfolk: North Barsham: North Barsham Parish Registers: Surnames of People who come from Other Parishes
  www.origins.org.uk/genuki/NFK/places/b/barsham_north/pr_strays.shtml

New Buckenham

- Norfolk: Guiltcross District: Buckenham, New
  www.genealogy.doun.org/transcriptions/
  Click on 'Parishes', 'B', & 'Buckenham New'. Includes Wesleyan Methodist baptisms 1812-37

North Elmham

- Norfolk: Mitford & Launditch District: Elmham, North
  www.genealogy.doun.org/transcriptions/
  Click on 'Parishes', 'E', & 'Elmham North'. Includes bishops' transcripts 1800-31

North Pickenham

- Norfolk: Swaffham District: Pickenham North
  www.genealogy.doun.org/transcriptions/
  Click on 'Parishes', 'P', & 'Pickenham North'. Includes baptisms, 1790-1835, & marriages 1813-36; also bishops' transcripts 1725-1817. Many years missing

North Runcton

- North Runcton Baptisms 1563-1812
  www.runctonweb.co.uk/hist/baptisms.html
  apling.freeservers.com/ParishRecords/NorthRunctonBaptisms.htm
- North Runcton Marriages 1653-1719
  apling.freeservers.com/ParishRecords/NorthRunctonMarriages1653-1719.htm
  Continued for 1719-74 on one further page
- North Runcton Marriages: Index of Marriages found in the Archdeacons' Transcripts for North Runcton, Norfolk, from 1740-1812
  contueor.com/wisbech/indexes/north_runcton.htm

North Tuddenham

- Norfolk: Mitford & Launditch District: North and West Tuddenham:
  www.genealogy.doun.org/transcriptions/
  Click on 'Parishes', 'N', & 'North and West Tuddenham'. Bishops' transcripts 1725-1811. Incomplete

Northwold

- Norfolk: Thetford District: Northwold
  www.genealogy.doun.org/transcriptions/
  Click on 'Parishes', 'N' & 'Northwold'. Includes bishops' transcripts, 1725-1812 (incomplete)

Norwich

- Norfolk: Norwich: Church of England
  www.origins.org.uk/genuki/NFK/places/n/norwich/church/c_of_e.shtml
  Includes citations to some published registers *etc.*
- Norfolk: Norwich District: Norwich St. Edmund
  www.genealogy.doun.org/transcriptions/
  Click on 'Parishes', 'N', & 'Norwich St. Edmund'. Includes baptisms, 1813-84, banns 1754-1901, marriages 1754-1885, & burials 1813-56. Incomplete
- Norfolk: Norwich District: Norwich St. Etheldred
  www.genealogy.doun.org/transcriptions/
  Click on 'Parishes', 'N', & 'Norwich St. Etheldred'. Includes marriages, 1755-1812. Incomplete
- Norfolk: Norwich District: Norwich St. Margaret
  www.genealogy.doun.org/transcriptions/
  Click on 'Parishes', 'N', & 'Norwich St. Margaret'. Includes baptisms, 1695-1728, marriages 1696-1800 & burials 1695-1701
- Norfolk: Norwich District: Norwich St. Martin at Oak
  www.genealogy.doun.org/transcriptions/
  Click on 'Parishes', 'N' & 'Norwich St. Martin at Oak'. Includes baptisms, 1813-19

Ormesby St. Margaret

- Norfolk: Flegg District: Ormesby St. Margaret w. Scratby
  www.genealogy.doun.org.transcriptions/
  Click on 'Parishes', 'O' & 'Ormesby St. Margaret w. Scratby'. Includes baptisms, 1787-1869, marriages 1813-37, & burials 1787-1867

Outwell

- Outwell Baptisms: Index of Baptisms found in the Archdeacons' Transcripts for Outwell, Norfolk, from 1725-1812
  contueor.com/wisbech/indexes/outwell_bp.htm
- Outwell Marriages: Index of Marriages found in the Archdeacons' Transcripts for Outwell, Norfolk, from 1725-1812
  contueor.com/wisbech/indexes/outwell.htm

- Outwell Burials: Index of selected burials found in the Archdeacons' Transcripts for Outwell, Norfolk from 1725-1812
  contueor.com/wisbech/indexes/outwell_br.htm

Oxborough
- Norfolk: Swaffham District: Oxborough
  www.genealogy.doun.org/transcriptions/
  Click on 'Parishes', 'O', & 'Oxborough'. Includes bishops' transcripts, 1726-1812 (some years missing)

Oxnead
- Norfolk: Aylsham District: Oxnead
  www.genealogy.doun.org/transcriptions/
  Click on 'Parishes', 'O' & 'Oxnead'. Includes bishops' transcripts 1630-1810 (many years missing)

Pentney
- Norfolk: Freebridge Lynn District: Pentney
  www.genealogy.doun.org/transcriptions/
  Click on 'Parishes', 'P', & 'Pentney'. Includes baptisms, 1730-1902, banns 1755-1903, marriages 1731-1903, & burials 1731-1902

Potter Heigham
- Norfolk: Tunstead & Happing District: Potter Heigham
  www.genealogy.doun.org/transcriptions/
  Click on 'Parishes', 'P', & 'Potter Heigham'. Includes baptisms 1645-1903, marriages 1626-1838, & burials 1627-1902; also bishops' transcripts 1817

Quiddenham
- Norfolk: Guiltcross District: Quiddenham
  www.genealogy.doun.org/transcriptions/
  Click on 'Parishes', 'Q', & 'Quiddenham'. Includes baptisms (bishops' transcripts), 1817 only

Reymerstone

Norfolk: Mitford & Launditch District: Reymerstone
www.genealogy.doun.org/transcriptions/
Click on 'Parishes', 'R', & 'Reymerstone'. Includes bishops' transcripts 1725-1812 (some years missing)

Ridlington
- Norfolk: Tunstead & Happing District: Ridlington
  www.genealogy.doun.org/transcriptions/
  Click on 'Parishes', 'R', & 'Ridlington'. Includes baptisms, 1559-1812, marriages 1559-1838, & burials 1559-1812. Incomplete

Rollesby
- Norfolk: Flegg District: Rollesby
  www.genealogy.doun.org/transcriptions/
  Click on 'Parishes', 'R', & 'Rollesby'. Includes baptisms, 1802-6

Ryburgh Magna
- Norfolk: Walsingham District: Ryburgh Magna
  www.genealogy.doun.org/transcriptions/
  Click on 'Parishes', 'R', & 'Ryburgh'. Includes baptisms, 1759-1832

Saham Toney
- Norfolk: Saham Toney: Saham Toney Parish Registers: List of Surnames of people who come from other Parishes
  www.origins.org.uk/genuki/NFK/places/s/saham_toney/pr_strays.shtml

Salhouse
- Norfolk: St. Faith's District: Salhouse
  www.genealogy.doun.org/transcriptions/
  Click on 'Parishes', 'S', & 'Salhouse'. Includes baptisms, 1722-1865, marriages 1722-1837 & burials 1723-1901. Also banns 1760-1823 (many years missing)

Santon
- Norfolk: Thetford District: Santon
  www.genealogy.doun.org/transcriptions/
  Click on 'Parishes', 'S', & 'Santon'. Includes bishops' transcripts of baptisms & burials, 1770-1802 (many years missing)

Saxlingham
- Norfolk: Walsingham District: Saxlingham
  www.genealogy.doun.org/transcriptions/
  Click on 'Parishes', 'S', & 'Saxlingham'. Includes baptisms, 1637-1902, marriages 1754-1912, & burials 1622-1812

Scratby
See Ormesby St. Margaret

Sherringham

- Norfolk: Erpingham District: Sherringham
  www.genealogy.doun.org/transcriptions/
  Click on 'Parishes', 'S', & 'Sheringham'. Includes baptisms, 1670-1812 (some years missing)

Shipdham

- Norfolk: Mitford & Launditch District: Shipdham
  www.genealogy.doun.org/transcriptions/
  Click on 'Parishes', 'S' & 'Shipdham'. Includes burials 1755; also bishops' transcripts 1725-1812 (incomplete)

Skeyton

- Norfolk: Aylsham District: Skeyton
  www.genealogy.doun.org/transcriptions/
  Click on 'Parishes', 'S' & 'Skeyton'. Includes bishops' transcripts 1670-1775 (many years missing)

Sloley

- Norfolk: Tunstead & Happing District: Sloley
  www.genealogy.doun.org/transcriptions/
  Click on 'Parishes', 'S' & 'Sloley'. Includes baptisms, 1813-70 & marriages 1750-1835. Incomplete

Smallburgh

- Norfolk: Tunstead & Happing District: Smallburgh
  www.genealogy.doun.org/transcrptions/
  Click on 'Parishes', 'S' & 'Smallburgh'. Includes baptisms, 1561-1863, banns 1759-1903, marriages 1561-1902, & burials 1561-1902. Incomplete

South Pickenham

- Norfolk: Swaffham District: Pickenham South
  www.genealogy.doun.org/transcriptions/
  Click on 'Parishes', 'P' & 'Pickenham South'. Includes bishops' transcripts 1726-1817 (many years missing)

Southacre

- Norfolk: Swaffham District: Southacre
  www.genealogy.doun.org/transcriptions/
  Click on 'Parishes', 'S' & 'Southacre'. Includes bishops' transcripts 1726-1812 (many years missing)

Southburgh

- Norfolk: Mitford & Launditch District: Southburgh
  www.genealogy.doun.org/transcriptions/
  Click on 'Parishes', 'S' & 'Southburgh'. Includes bishops' transcripts, 1725-1812. Some years missing (especially burials)

Southery

- Southery (South Ferry) Marriages: Index of Marriages found in the Archdeacons' Transcripts for Southery (South Ferry), Norfolk, from 1725-1812
  contueor.com/wisbech/indexes/southery.htm

Spixworth

- Norfolk: St. Faith's District: Spixworth
  www.genealogy.doun.org/transcriptions/
  Click on 'Parishes', 'S' & 'Spixworth'. Includes baptisms, 1763-1902, banns 1838-52, marriages 1754-1832, & burials 1750-1812. Many years missing

Sporle with Palgrave

- Norfolk: Swaffham District: Sporle with Palgrave
  www.genealogy.doun.org/transcriptions/
  Click on 'Parishes', 'S' & 'Sporle with Palgrave'. Includes bishops' transcripts 1725-1812 (many years missing)

Sprowston

Norfolk: St. Faith's District: Sprowston
www.genealogy.doun.org/transcriptions/
Click on 'Parishes', 'S' & 'Sprowston'. Includes baptisms, 1673-1904, marriages 1764-1903, & burials 1721-1902. Incomplete

Stalham

- Norfolk: Tunstead & Happing District: Stalham
  www.genealogy.doun.org/transcriptions/
  Click on 'Parishes', 'S' & 'Stalham'. Includes marriages 1723-1812 (incomplete)

Stanford

- Norfolk: Swaffham District: Stanford
  www.genealogy.doun.org/transcriptions/
  Click on 'Parishes', 'S' & 'Stanford'. Includes bishops' transcripts 1725-1811. Many years missing

Starston

- Norfolk: Depwade District: Starston
  www.genealogy.doun.org/transcriptions/
  Click on 'Parishes', 'S' & 'Starston'. Includes bishops' transcripts for marriages & burials, 1789-1811 (incomplete)

Stiffkey

- Norfolk: Walsingham District: Stiffkey
  www.genealogy.doun.org/transcriptions/
  Click on 'Parishes', 'S' & 'Stiffkey'. Includes baptisms, 1813-65, banns 1758-1812, marriages 1754-1901, & burials 1813-1902. Incomplete

Stow Bardolph

- Stow Bardolph Marriages: Index of Marriages found in the Archdeacons' Transcripts for Stow Bardolph, Norfolk, from 1725-1812
  contueor.com/wisbech/indexes/stow_bardolph.htm

Stratton Strawless

- Norfolk: Aylsham District: Stratton Strawless
  www.genealogy.doun.org/transcriptions/
  Click on 'Parishes', 'S' & 'Stratton Strawless'. Includes baptisms 1620-1812, marriages, 1620-1901, & burials 1695-1765 (incomplete); also bishops' transcripts 1695-1765 (many years missing)

Suffield

- Norfolk: Erpingham Distirct: Suffield
  www.genealogy.doun.org/transcriptions/
  Click on 'Parishes', 'S', & 'Suffield'. Includes marriages 1558-1648. Some years missing

Swanton Morley

- Norfolk: Mitford & Launditch District: Swanton Morley
  www.genealogy.doun.org/transcriptions/
  Click on 'Parishes', 'S' & 'Swanton Morley'. Includes burials 1678-1738; also bishops' transcripts 1752

Swanton Novers

- Swanton Novers, Norfolk, England: Surnames from Entries of births/baptisms and deaths/burials 1895-1933 recorded by William Ducker, Parish Clerk
  ww3.telus.net/swanton_novers/willddiary.htm

Terrington St. Clement

- Terrington St. Clement Baptisms: Index of selected baptisms found in both the parish register and Archdeacons' Transcripts for Terrington St. Clement, Norfolk, from 1671-1848
  contueor.com/wisbech/indexes/terrington_st_c.bp.htm

- Terrington St. Clemetn Marriages: Index of Marriages found in both the parish register and Archdeacons' Transcripts for Terrington St. Clement, Norfolk, from 1598-1599, 1651-1655 & 1671-1830
  contueor.com/wisbech/indexes/terrington_st_c.htm

- Terrington St. Clement Burials: Index of selected burials found in both the parish registers and Archdeacons' transcripts for Terrington St. Clement, Norfolk, from 1671-1812 and the Parish Register from 1846-1931
  contueor.com/wisbech/indexes/terrington_st_clement_br.htm

Terrington St. John

- Terrington St. John Marriages: Index of Marriages found in the Archdeacons' Transcripts for Terrington St. John, Norfolk, from 1701-1812
  contueor.com/wisbech/indexes/terrington_st_j.htm

Thetford

- Norfolk: Thetford District: Thetford St. Mary's
  www.genealogy.doun.org/transcriptions/
  Includes baptisms 1640-1902, banns 1754-1902, marriages 1653-1902, & burials 1653-1902. Incomplete

- Norfolk: Thetford: Thetford St. Mary's Parish Registers: List of People who come from other parishes
  www.origins.org.uk/NFK/places/t/thetford/mary/pr_strays.shtml

Thornage

- Norfolk: Erpingham District: Thornage
  www.genealogy.doun.org/transcriptions/
  Click on 'Parishes', 'T' & 'Thornage'. Includes baptisms, 1743-1812, marriages 1744-53, & burials 1744-1812

Tibenham

- Norfolk: Tibenham: Tibenham Parish Registers: List of Surnames of people who come from other parishes
  www.origins.org.uk/genuki/NFK/places/t/tibenham/pr_strays.shtml

- Norfolk: Tibenham: List of Surnames in the Tibenham Baptism Registers 1813-1858
  www.origins.org.uk/genuki/NFK/places/t/tibenham/pr_bapt_names.shtml

Tilney All Saints

- Norfolk: Wisbech District: Tilney All Saints
  www.genealogy.doun.org/transcriptions/
  Click on 'Parishes', 'T' & 'Tilney All Saints'. Includes baptisms, 1680-1902 & burials 1678-1919

- Tilney All Saints Marriages: Index of Marriages found in the Archdeacons' Transcripts for Tilney All Saints, Norfolk, from 1706-1812
  contueor.com/wisbech/indexes/tilney_all_saints.htm

Tilney cum Islington

- Norfolk: Wisbech District: Tilney cum Islington
  www.genealogy.doun.org/transcriptions/
  Click on 'Parishes', 'T' & 'Tilney cum Islington'. Includes baptisms, 1675-1899, marriages 1559-1902, & burials 1571-1943. Incomplete

- Tilney cum Islington Marriages: Index of Marriages found in the Archdeacons' Transcripts for Tilney cum Islington, Norfolk, from 1668-1812
  contueor.com/wisbech/indexes/tilney_Islington.htm

Tilney St. Lawrence

- Tilney St. Lawrence Marriages: Index of Marriages found in the Archdeacons' transcripts for Tilney St. Lawrence, Norfolk, from 1707-1727 & 1750-1812
  contueor.còm.wisbech/indexes/tilney_st_law.htm

Trunch

- Trunch Family History Pages
  www.trunchnorfolk.cwc.net/family.htm
  Includes baptisms 1725-50 & 1800-1912, marriages 1725-1812 and burials 1725-1750, *etc.*

- Norfolk: Erpingham District: Trunch
  www.genealogy.doun.org/transcriptions/
  Click on 'Parishes', 'T' & 'Trunch'. Includes baptisms, 1800-1812, & marriages 1800-1812; also marriages from bishops' transcripts 1725-99 (incomplete)

Tunstead

- Norfolk: Tunstead & Happing District: Tunstead
  www.genealogy.doun.org/transcriptions/
  Click on 'Parishes', 'T' & 'Tunstead'. Includes baptisms 1813-1901, marriages 1754-1902, & burials 1735-1908. Incomplete

Walcot

- Norfolk: Tunstead & Happing District: Walcot
  www.genealogy.doun.org/transcriptions/
  Click on 'Parishes', 'W' & 'Walcot'. Includes baptisms 1813-1904 & marriages 1754-1902. Incomplete

Walpole St. Andrew

- Walpole St. Andrew Marriages: Index of Marriages found in the Parish Register for Walpole St. Andrew, Norfolk, from 1654-1823, plus additional selected marriages and banns from 1824-1894
  contueor.com/wisbech/indexes/walpole_a.htm

Walpole St. Peter

- Walpole St. Peter Marriages: Index of Marriages found in the Archdeacons' Trnascripts for Walpole St. Peter, Norfolk, from 1704-1812
  contueor.com/wisbech/indexes/walpole_p.htm

Walsoken

- Walsoken Baptisms: Index of selected baptisms found in the Archdeacons' Transcripts for Walsoken, Norfolk, from 1668-1812, including all baptisms from 1770-1800, as well as a dozen entries from the parish register
contueor.com/wisbech/indexes/walsoken_bp.htm

- Walsoken Marriages: Index of Marriages found in the Archdeacons' Transcripts for Walsoken, Norfolk from 1668-1812
contueor.com/wisbech/indexes/walsoken.htm

- Walsoken Burials: Index of selected burials found in the Archdeacons' Transcripts for Walsoken, Norfolk from 1668-1812, including all burials from 1770-1800 as well as a dozen entries from the parish register
contueor.com/wisbech/indexes/walsoken_br.htm

Warham All Saints

- Norfolk: Walsingham District: Warham All Saints
www.genealogy.doun.org/transcriptions/
Click on 'Parishes', 'W' & 'Warham All Saints'. Includes baptisms, 1799-1893, banns 1754-1812, marriages 1754-1812 & burials 1799-1902. Incomplete

Waterden

- Norfolk: Docking District: Waterden
www.genealogy.doun.org/transcriptions/
Click on 'Parishes', 'W' & 'Waterden'. Includes marriages, 1743-1811 (many years missing)

Weasenham All Saints

- Norfolk: Mitford & Launditch District: Weasenham All Saints or Upper
www.genealogy.doun.org/transcriptions/
Click on 'Parishes', 'W' & 'Weasenham All Saints or Upper'. Includes baptisms 1637-1812, marriages 1703-1812, & burials 1642-1812. Incomplete

Weeting with Broomhill

- Norfolk: Thetford District: Weeting with Broomhill
www.genealogy.doun.org/transcriptions/
Click on 'Parishes', 'W' & 'Weeting with Broomhill'. Includes bishops' transcripts, 1726-1812. Incomplete

Westbourne

- Norfolk: Forehoe District: Welbourne
www.genealogy.doun.org/transcriptions/
Click on 'Parishes', 'W' & 'Welbourne'. Includes bishops' transcripts 1725-1811 (many years missing)

West Beckham

- Norfolk: Erpingham District: West Beckham
www.genealogy.doun.org/transcriptions/
Click on 'Parishes', 'W' & 'West Beckham'. Includes baptisms, 1867-1900, from the workhouse register

West Lynn

- West Lynn Marriages: Index of Marriages found in the Archdeacons' Transcripts for West Lynn, Norfolk from 1730-1812
contueor.com/wisbech/indexes/west_lynn.htm

West Rudham

- Norfolk: Docking District: West Rudham
www.genealogy.doun.org/transcriptions/
Click on 'Parishes', 'W' & 'West Rudham'. Includes baptisms 1729-1867, marriages 1730-1836, & burials 1729-1847

West Somerton

- Norfolk: Flegg District: West Somerton
www.genealogy.doun.org/transcriptions/index.php
Click on 'Parishes', 'W' & 'West Somerton'. Includes baptisms, 1813-94

West Tofts

- Norfolk Thetford District: West Tofts
www.genealogy.doun.org/transcriptions/
Click on 'Parishes', 'W' & 'West Tofts'. Includes bishops' transcripts, 1725-1812 (many years missing)

West Tuddenham

See North Tuddenham

West Walton

- West Walton Marriages: Index of Marriages found in the Archdeacons' Transcripts from 1740-1812, combined with an index of selected marriages found in the parish register from 1662-1835
contueor.com/wisbech/indexes/west_walton.htm

Westfield

- Norfolk: Mitford & Launditch District: Westfield
  www.genealogy.doun.org/transcriptions/
  Click on 'Parishes', 'W', & Westfield'. Includes bishops' transcripts, 1725-1812. Some years missing (especially marriages)

Westwick

- Norfolk: Tunstead & Happing District: Westwick
  www.genealogy.doun.org/transcriptions/
  Click on 'Parishes', 'W' & 'Westwick'. Includes baptisms, 1790-1812, marriages 1754-1836 & burials 1790-99. Incomplete

Whinburgh

- Norfolk: Mitford & Launditch District: Whinburgh
  www.genealogy.doun.org/transcriptions/
  Click on 'Parishes', 'W', & 'Whinburgh'. Includes bishops' transcripts, 1725-1811 (many years missing)

Wiggenhall St. Mary Magdalen

- Wiggenhall St. Mary Magdalen Marriages: Index of Marriages found in the Archdeacons' Transcripts for Wiggenhall St. Mary Magdalen, Norfolk, from 1744-1805
  contueor.com/wisbech/indexes/wiggenhall_m_m.htm

Wiggenhall St. Mary the Virgin

- Wiggenhall St. Mary the Virgin Marriages: Index of Marriages found in the Parish Register for Wiggenhall St. Mary the Virgin, Norfolk from 1669-1822
  contueor.com/wisbech/indexes/wiggenhall_st_mary_the_virgin.htm

Wiggenhall St. Peter

- Wiggenhall St. Peter Marriages: Index of Marriages found in the Archdeacons' Transcripts for Wiggenhall St. Peter, Norfolk, from 1744-1805
  contueor.com/wisbech/indexes/wiggenhall_p.htm

Wilton

- Norfolk: Thetford District: Wilton
  www.genealogy.doun.org/transcriptions/
  Click on 'Parishes', 'W' & 'Wilton'. Includes baptisms, 1634-5 & 1640, marriages 1634-5, & burials 1634-5

Winfarthing

- Norfolk: Winfarthing: Winfarthing Parish Registers: People who come from other parishes
  www.origins.org.uk/genuki/NFK/places/w/winfarthing/pr_strays.shtml

Winterton

- Norfolk: Flegg District: Winterton with East Somerton
  www.genealogy.doun.org/transcriptions/
  Click on 'Parishes', 'W' & 'Winterton with East Somerton'. Includes baptisms, 1765-1842, marriages 1747-1901, & burials 1813-1902

Witton

Norfolk: Tunstead & Happing District: Witton
www.genealogy.doun.org/transcriptions/
Click on 'Parishes', 'W' & 'Witton'. Includes bishops' transcripts, 1725-80 (incomplete)

Worstead

- Norfolk: Tunstall & Happing District: Worstead
  www.genealogy.doun.org/transcriptions/
  Click on 'Parishes', 'W' & 'Worstead'. Includes baptisms, 1661-1840, marriages 1662-1899, & burials 1661-1884. Incomplete

Wramplingham

- Norfolk: Forehoe District: Wramplingham
  www.genealogy.doun.org/transcriptions/
  Click on 'Parishes', 'W' & 'Wramplingham'. Includes bishops' transcripts, 1725-1811 (many years missing)

Wroxham

- Norfolk: St. Faith's District: Wroxham
  www.genealogy.doun.org/transcriptions/
  Click on 'Parishes, 'W' & 'Wroxham'. Includes baptisms, 1742-1901, banns 1761-1901, marriages 1754-1836, & burials 1742-1900. Incomplete

Northamptonshire

Civil Registration

- Registration Districts in Northamptonshire
  www.fhsc.org.uk/genuki/REG/nth.htm
  Between 1837 and 1930

Parish & Non-Parochial Registers: Introductory Pages & Lists

- Parish Registers
  www.nthgenuki.org.uk
  Scroll down and click on 'Records' and 'Anglican Parish Registers'. Lists registers held by Northamptonshire Record Office. There is also a page listing 'Non-Anglican registers'

- Northamptonshire
  www.sog.org.uk/prc/northampton.html
  Parish registers, printed, typescript, *etc.,* in the library of the Society of Genealogists

- Quaker Family History Society: Northamptonshire
  www.rootsweb.com/~engqfhs/Research/counties/northants.htm
  Notes on Quaker records

Indexes

- National Burial Index (Northamptonshire Family History Society)
  www.familyhistoryonline.co.uk/database/NBINorthantsFHS.shtml
  Pay per view

- IGI Batch Numbers for Northampton, England
  freepages.genealogy.rootsweb.com/~hughwallis/IGIBatchNumbers/CountyNorthampton.htm

- Northamptonshire, England: Parish and Probate Records
  www.ancestry.com/search/db.aspx?dbid=5915

Transcript Collections on the Web

- Northants Transcripts
  www.stevejgarton.co.uk/

- Other Northants & Hunts Parish Register Extracts
  freepages.genealogy.rootsweb.com/~maureenbryon/id82.htm
  Brief extracts from many registers, not otherwise listed here

Apethorpe

- Apethorpe Baptisms 1800-1813
  www.stevejgarton.co.uk/NT.htm
  Click on title. Index

- Apethorpe Marriages 1754-1812
  www.stevejgarton.co.uk/NT.htm
  Click on title. Continued to 1837 on one further page

- Apethorpe Burials 1740 onwards
  www.stevejgarton.co.uk/NT.htm
  Click on title. Index

Benefield

- Benefield Parish Register Extracts
  freepages.genealogy.rootsweb.com/~maureenbryson/id47
  Extracts only 1570-1741

Castor

- Castor Register 1538-1740
  www.thearchive.org.uk/register/regintro.htm
  In progress

Clapton

- Clapton Parish Register Extracts
  freepages.genealogy.rootsweb.com/~maureenbryson/id83.htm
  Extracts only, 1558-1812

Cold Higham

- Cold Higham, Northamptonshire, England: Christening Records
  freepages.genealogy.rootsweb.com/~coleen/cold_higham.html
  Covers 1813-28. For continuations, see:
  1828-49 **/ch2.htm** 1849-69 **/ch3.html**
  1869-93 **/ch4.html**

- Cold Higham, Northamptonshire, England: Marriage Records 1813-1835
  freepages.genealogy.rootsweb.com/~coleen/chmarriages.html

Collyweston

- Collyweston Parish Register Extracts
  freepages.genealogy.rootsweb.com/~maureenbryson/id74.htm
  Extracts only, 16-18th c.

Gretton

- Gretton Parish Register Extracts
  freepages.genealogy.rootsweb.com/~maureenbryson/id59.htm
  Extracts only, 1560-1837

- Gretton Parish Records
  www.maurice.skynet.co.uk/genuki/big/eng/NTH/jorda.htm
  Lookups offered

Kings Cliffe

- Kings Cliffe Parish Register Extracts
  freepages.genealogy.rootsweb.com/~maureenbryson/id60.htm
  Extracts only, 1629-1853

Kingsthorpe

- Kingsthorpe Church Records
  www.maurice.skynet.co.uk/genuki/big/eng/NTH/Kingsthorpe/
  Lookups offered

Luddington

- Luddington Parish Register Extracts
  freepages.genealogy.rootsweb.com/~maureenbryson/id61.htm
  Extracts only, 1682-1866

Naseby

- Naseby Baptisms, 1813-1864
  www.stevejgarton.co.uk/NT.htm
  Click on title

Oundle

- Baptismal Register for Oundle, Northamptonshire, 1813-1838
  uk-transcriptions.accessgenealogy.com/Oundle%20BapReg(Year).htm
  For index, see **/Oundle%20BapReg(surname).htm**

- Oundle Baptisms 1813-1818
  uk-transcriptions.accessgenealogy.com/OundleBapts.htm

- Oundle Parish Register Extracts
  freepages.genealogy.rootsweb.com/~maureenbryson/id49.htm
  Extracts only, 1625-1840

Pattishall

- Pattishall, Northamptonshire, England: Marriage Records Transcribed from Latter Day Saints Microfiche
  freepages.genealogy.rootsweb.com/~coleen/pattishall.html
  Covers 1837-84. For 1884-1924 see **/pattishalltwo.html**

Potterspury

- Potterspury Parish Records
  www.potterspury.org.uk/fhs/parishrecords.htm
  Click on 'genealogy' for marriages 1700-1837 & burials 1812-66

Stanion

- Stanion Parish Register Extracts
  freepages.genealogy.rootsweb.com/~maureenbryson/id62.htm
  Extracts only, 1668-1787

Tansor

- Tansor Parish Register Extracts
  freepages.genealogy.rootsweb.com/~maureenbryson/id73.htm
  Extracts only, 1639-1796

Thrapston

- Thrapston Parish Register Extracts
  freepages.genealogy.rootsweb.com/~maureenbryson/id78.htm
  Extracts only, 1653-1802

Titchmarsh

Titchmarsh Parish Register Extracts
freepages.genealogy.rootsweb.com/~maureenbryson/id81.htm
Extracts only, 1630-1853

Twywell

- Twywell Parish Register Extracts
  freepages.genealogy.rootsweb.com/~maureenbryson/id72.htm
  Extracts only, 1626-1880

Walgrave

- Transcript of Baptisms in Walgrave 1710-1878 for persons aged 1+
  website.lineone.net/~stevejgarton/WBPT.htm

Welford

- Welford Baptisms 1813-1839
  www.stevejgarton.co.uk/NT.htm
  Click on title

Wellingborough

- Wellingborough All Hallows (Northamptonshire) Parish Registers for 1812
  www.stepback.co.uk/page11.html

Wilbarston

- Wilbarston Parish Register Extracts
  freepages.genealogy.rootsweb.com/~maureenbryson/id76.htm
  Extracts only, 1707-1811

Northumberland

See also Durham

Civil Registration

- Registration Districts in Northumberland
  www.fhsc.org.uk/genuki/REG/nbl.htm
  Between 1837 and 1930

- Northumberland: Civil Registration
  www.genuki.bpears.org.uk/genuki/NBL/CivilRegistration.html
  Links to addresses of each registration office

- Newcastle Register Office Indexes
  www.ndfhs.org.uk/RegIndex.html
  Indexes to civil registers of births and marriages

- [St. Catherine's House Marriage Index, Jan-March, 1849. District 25. Northumberland/Westmoreland]
  www.cs.ncl.ac.uk/genuki/StCathsTranscriptions/CATH4925.TXT

- Cumbrian Genealogy: The St. Catherine's Marriage Index for March Quarter 1849
  janelittle.members.beeb.net/Miscellaneous/StCatsMarchQr1849Marriages.html
  For Northumberland and Westmoreland

Parish & Non-Parochial Registers: Introductory Pages & Lists

- Northumberland Church Records
  www.genuki.bpears.org.uk/NBL/ChurchRecords.html
  Links page

- Northumberland Archive Service. Diocese of Newcastle: Anglican Parish Registers
  www.swinhope.myby.co.uk/NROParishRecords.html
  List

- Northumberland Archive Service Methodist Registers
  www.swinhope.myby.co.uk/NRO/MethRecords.html

- Northumberland Archive Service. Presbyterian and Congregational Registers
www.swinhope.myby.co.uk/NRO/UReform.html

- Northumberland Archive Service. Roman Catholic Registers
www.swinhope.myby.co.uk/NRO/RCatholic.html

- Northumberland Archive Service. Registers of other Denominations.
www.swinhope.myby.co.uk/NRO/OtherDenoms.htm

- Northumberland Archive Service. Civil Cemetery Records
www.swinhope.myby.co.uk/NRO/Cemeteries.html

- Newcastle upon Tyne City Libraries & Arts. Local Studies Library. Genealogy guide no. 5. Parish Register Transcripts and Indexes
www.genuki.bpears.org.uk/NBL/NCLLib/NCLGG5.html
Includes some Co. Durham registers

- Northumberland Archive Service: Transcripts in Berwick upon Tweed Record Office.
www.swinhope.myby.co.uk/NRO/Berwick.html
Of parish registers, monumental inscriptions, *etc.*

- Tyne & Wear Archives User Guides
www.thenortheast.com/archives/guides.html
Includes guides to 'Parish Registers on Microfilm', 'Roman Catholic Registers' 'Methodist Registers', 'Registers of other denominations', *etc.* The area covered includes Gateshead, Newcastle, North Tyneside, South Tyneside and Sunderland

- Durham County Record Office. Handlist 7. Northumberland and North Yorkshire Transcripts and Indexes (Church of England
www.durham.gov.uk/recordoffice/usp.nsf/lookup/pdfhandlists/$file/handlist07.pdf

- Library Catalogue
www.ndfhs.fsnet.co.uk/Catalogue.pdf
Parish register transcripts and indexes in the Library of the Northumberland & Durham Family History Society

- Northumberland & Durham Family History Society: Transcripts on Computer at Bolbec Hall. Part 2. Northumberland
www.ndfhs.org.uk/Transcripts_NBL.html
List of parish register transcripts

- Northumberland
www.sog.org.uk/prc/northumberland.html
Parish registers, printed, typescript, *etc.,* in the library of the Society of Genealogists

- Quaker Family History Society: Northumberland
www.rootsweb.com/~engqfhs/Research/counties/nortum.htm
Notes on Quaker records

Indexes

- Northumberland and Durham Baptisms
www.familyhistoryonline.co.uk/database/DFHSbaps.shtml
Pay per view index

- National Burial Index (Northumberland and Durham Family History Society)
www.familyhistoryonline.co.uk/database/NBINDFHS.shtml
Pay per view

- Free Reg: Northumberland
freereg.rootsweb.com/parishes/nbl/index.htm
Details of the registers currently included in a project to index births, deaths and marriages

- Boyd's Marriage Index: Parishes and Periods of Records: Northumberland
www.britishorigins.com/help/popup-aboutbo-bmi-countydetails.htm
Click on 'Northumberland'

- IGI Batch Numbers for Northumberland, England
freepages.genealogy.rootsweb.com/~hughwallis/IGIBatchNumbers/CountyNorthumberland.htm

Publications

- Northumberland & Durham Family History Society Publications on Microfiche
www.ndfhs.org.uk/FichePriceList.pdf
Includes parish registers, monumental inscriptions, *etc.*

- Northfiche: Northumberland Parish Register Transcripts & Indexes
  www.jwillans.freeserve.co.uk/northficnbl.html
  Fiche for sale

- Northumberland Record Office: Microfiche for Sale
  www.swinhope.myby.co.uk/NRO/Fiche.pdf
  Includes many registers

- Original Indexes
  www.original-indexes.demon.co.uk
  Many transcripts and indexes for Northumberland, Co. Durham, & North Yorkshire

Allendale
See also Carrshield

- Allendale Church Records
  www.genuki.bpears.org.uk/NBL/Allendale/ChurchRecords.html
  List with locations

Alwinton
- Alwinton: Church Records
  www.genuki.bpears.org.uk/NBL/Alwinton/ChurchRecords.html

Bedlington
- Marriages from the Registers of Bedlington (1813-1837)
  www.cs.ncl.ac.uk/genuki/Transcriptions/NBL/MBED.html

Belford
- Belford Baptisms 1813-1837
  www.cs.ncl.ac.uk/genuki/Transcriptions/NBL/XBFD.html

Blanchland
- Marriages from the Blanchland Registers (1753-1837)
  www.cs.ncl.ac.uk/genuki/Transcriptions/NBL/BLA.html

Bothal
- Marriages from the Registers of Bothal (1813-1837)
  www.cs.ncl.ac.uk/genuki/Transcriptions/NBL/MBOT.html

Bywell St. Andrew
- Marriages from the Bywell St Andrew Registers (1686-1837)
  www.cs.ncl.ac.uk/genuki/Transcriptions/NBL/BSA.html

Bywell St. Peter
- Marriages from the Bywell St Peter Registers (1663-1837)
  www.cs.ncl.ac.uk/genuki/Transcriptions/NBL/BSP.html

Carrshield
- Baptisms from the Registers of Carrshield (1823-1837)
  www.cs.ncl.ac.uk/genuki/Transcriptions/NBL/XCSH.html
  In Allendale parish

Cramlington
- Marriages from the Registers of Cramlington (1814-1836)
  www.cs.ncl.ac.uk/genuki/Transcriptions/NBL/MCRA.html

Earsdon
- Selected Entries from Earsdon Registers 1626-1750
  www.genuki.bpears.org.uk/genuki/NBL/Earsdon/EarsReg.html
  From Craster's *History of Northumberland,* originally published 1909

- Marriages from the Registers of Earsdon (1813-1837)
  www.cs.ncl.ac.uk/genuki/Transcriptions/NBL/MEAR.html

Felton
- Felton and Swarland Local History Society Publications
  www.genuki.bpears.org.uk/NBL/Felton/LHS.html
  Includes some birth, marriage & death records for Felton area

Gosforth
- Marriages from the Registers of Gosforth (1813-1837)
  www.cs.ncl.ac.uk/genuki/Transcriptions/NBL/MGOS.html

Halton
- Baptisms from the Registers of Halton (1813-1837)
  www.cs.ncl.ac.uk/genuki/Transcriptions/NBL/XHAL.html

- Marriages from the Halton Registers (1654-1769)
  www.cs.ncl.ac.uk/genuki/Transcriptions/NBL/HAL.html

Haydon Bridge
- Marriages from the Registers of Haydon Bridge (1813-1837)
  www.cs.ncl.ac.uk/genuki/Transcriptions/NBL/MHBR.html

Hebburn

- Marriages from the Registers of Hebburn (1813-1836)
  www.cs.ncl.ac.uk/genuki/Transcriptions/NBL/MHEB.html

Heddon on the Wall

- Historical Records for the 1800's from the *Old Bywell* church reader
  www.heddon.currantbun.com/history/records/bmd.htm
  Heddon on the Wall births, marriages & deaths, 1888-90

Hexham

- Marriages from the Hexham Registers (1540-1599)
  www.cs.ncl.ac.uk/genuki/Transcriptions/NBL/HEX1540.html
  Continued as follows:
  1600-1699 **/HEX1600.html** 1700-1749 **/HEX1700.html**
  1750-1799 **/HEX1750.html** 1800-1837 **/HEX1800.html**

Holy Island

- Baptisms from the Registers of Holy Island (1813-1837)
  www.cs.ncl.ac.uk/genuki/Transcriptions/NBL/XHIS.html

- Burials from the Holy Island Registers (1813-1837)
  www.cs.ncl.ac.uk/genuki/Transcriptions/NBL/BHIS.html

Horton

- Marriages from the Horton Registers (1665-1837)
  www.cs.ncl.ac.uk/genuki/Transcriptions/NBL/HOR.html

Kirkhaugh

- Marriages from the Kirkhaugh Registers (1761-1837)
  www.cs.ncl.ac.uk/genuki/Transcriptions/NBL/KHG.html

Knaresdale

- Marriages from the Knaresdale Registers (1701-1837)
  www.cs.ncl.ac.uk/genuki/Transcriptions/NBL/KND.html

Lambley

- Marriages from the Lambley Registers (1743-1836)
  www.cs.ncl.ac.uk/genuki/Transcriptions/NBL/LBY.html

Longbenton

Baptisms from the Registers of Longbenton (1813-1821)
www.cs.ncl.ac.uk/genuki/Transcriptions/NBL/XLBN1813.html
Continued as follows:
1822-1829 **/XLBN1822.html** 1830-1837 **/XLBN1830.html**

- Marriages from the Longbenton Registers (1653-1799)
  www.cs.ncl.ac.uk/genuki/Transcriptions/NBL/LBN1653.html
  Continued to 1837 at **/LBN1800.html**

- Burials from the Longbenton Registers (1813-1826)
  www.cs.ncl.ac.uk/genuki/Transcriptions/NBL/BLBN1813.html
  Continued to 1837 at **/BLBN1827.html**

Matfen

- Matfen Marriages, 1846-1901
  www.cs.ncl.ac.uk/genuki/Transcriptions/NBL/Matfen.html
  In Stamfordham parish

Mitford

- Marriages from the Registers of Mitford (1813-1836)
  www.cs.ncl.ac.uk/genuki/Transcriptions/NBL/MMIT.html

Morpeth

- Marriages from the Registers of Morpeth (1813-1837)
  www.cs.ncl.ac.uk/genuki/Transcriptions/NBL/MMOR.html

Netherwitton

- Some Netherwitton Baptisms 1805-6
  www.jwillans.freeserve.co.uk/sample.html
  Facsimile of original register

Newburn

- Marriages from the Newburn Registers (1659-1799)
  www.cs.ncl.ac.uk/genuki/Transcriptions/NBL/NBN1659.html
  Continued to 1837 at **/NBN1800.html**

Newcastle Upon Tyne

- Marriages from the Newcastle Courant 1841
  www.cs.ncl.ac.uk/genuki/Transcriptions/NBL/MCOUR1841.html

- Newcastle-upon-Tyne: Records of Non-Conformist Churches and Congregations
  www.genuki.bpears.org.uk/genuki/NBL/Newcastle/nonconf.html
  Extensive list

- Burials at Newcastle General Cemetery, 1836-1837
  www.cs.ncl.ac.uk/genuki/Transcriptions/NBL/BNGC.html
  Register

- Marriages from the Newcastle St Andrew Registers (1589-1599)
  www.cs.ncl.ac.uk/genuki/Transcriptions/NBL/NSA1589.html
  Continued as follows:

1600-1649	**/NSA1600.html**	1650-1699	**/NSA1650.html**
1700-1749	**/NSA1700.html**	1750-1799	**/NSA1750.html**
1800-1824	**/NSA1800.html**	1825-1837	**/NSA1825.html**

- Baptisms from the Registers of Newcastle, St Ann (1813-1835)
  www.cs.ncl.ac.uk/genuki/Transcriptions/NBL/XNAN.html

- Burials from the Registers of Newcastle, St Ann (1828-1837)
  www.cs.ncl.ac.uk/genuki/Transcriptions/NBL/BNAN.html

- Marriages from the Registers of St John (1813-1823)
  www.cs.ncl.ac.uk/genuki/Transcriptions/NBL/MNSJ1813.html
  In Newcastle. Continued as follows:

1824-1828	**MNSJ1824.html**	1829-1833	**MNSJ1829.html**
1834-1837	**MNSJ1834.html**		

- Marriages from the Registers of St Nicholas (1813-1837)
  www.cs.ncl.ac.uk/genuki/Transcriptions/NBL/MNSN.html

North Shields
- Deaths and Fatal Injuries at North Shields on May 3rd 1941
  www.genuki.bpears.org.uk/genuki/NBL/Tynemouth/Shelter.html
  Air-raid deaths

Ovingham
- Baptisms from the Registers of Ovingham (1813-1837)
  www.cs.ncl.ac.uk/genuki/Transcriptions/NBL/XOVI.html

- Marriages from the Ovingham Registers (1679-1769)
  www.cs.ncl.ac.uk/genuki/Transcriptions/NBL/OVI.html
  Continued to 1837 at **/OVI1770.html**

- Burials from the registers of Ovingham (1813-1837)
  www.cs.ncl.ac.uk/genuki/Transcriptions/NBL/BOVI.html

Ponteland
- Marriages from the Registers of Ponteland (1813-1837)
  www.cs.ncl.ac.uk/genuki/Transcriptions/NBL/MPON.html

Rennington
- Burials from the Registers of Rennington (1813-1837)
  www.cs.ncl.ac.uk/genuki/Transcriptions/NBL/BREN.html

Rock
- Baptisms from the Registers of Rock (1813-1837)
  www.cs.ncl.ac.uk/genuki/Transcriptions/NBL/XROC.html

- Burials from the Registers of Rock (1813-1837)
  www.cs.ncl.ac.uk/genuki/Transcriptions/NBL/BROC.html

Shotley
- Marriages from the Shotley Registers (1670-1837)
  www.cs.ncl.ac.uk/genuki/Transcriptions/NBL/SHL.html

Slaley
- Marriages from the Slaley Registers (1725-1837)
  www.cs.ncl.ac.uk/genuki/Transcriptions/NBL/SLA.html

Stamfordham
See Matfen

Tynemouth
- Tynemouth Parish: Records of Non-Conformist Churches and Congregations
  www.genuki.bpears.org.uk/genuki/NBL/Tynemouth/tynnconf.html
  List with locations

- Marriages from the Registers of Tynemouth (1607-1679)
  www.cs.ncl.ac.uk/genuki/Transcriptions/NBL/MTYN1607.html
  Continued as follows:

1680-1719	**/MTYN1680.html**	1720-1754	**/MTYN1720.html**
1813-1821	**/MTYN1813.html**	1822-1829	**/MTYN1822.html**
1830-1837	**/MTYN1830.html**		

- Tynemouth Society of Friends: Burials 1661-1818
  www.cs.ncl.ac.uk/genuki/Transcriptions/NBL/BTYN-SoF.html

Ulgham
- Marriages from the Registers of Ulgham (1755-1834)
  www.cs.ncl.ac.uk/genuki/Transcriptions/NBL/MULG.html

Wallsend

- Marriages from the Registers of Wallsend (1813-1837)
  www.cs.ncl.ac.uk/genuki/Transcriptions/NBL/MWAL.html

Warden

- Marriages from the Registers of Warden (1813-1837)
  www.cs.ncl.ac.uk/genuki/Transcriptions/NBL/MWDN.html
- Burials from the Warden Registers (1813-1901)
  www.cs.ncl.ac.uk/genuki/Transcriptions/NBL/BWDN.html

Whitfield

- Marriages from the Whitfield Registers (1606-1837)
  www.cs.ncl.ac.uk/genuki/Transcriptions/NBL/WTF.html

Widdrington

- Marriages from the Registers of Widdrington (1826-1837)
  www.cs.ncl.ac.uk/genuki/Transcriptions/NBL/MWID.html

Woodhorn

- Marriages from the Registers of Woodhorn (1813-1839)
  www.cs.ncl.ac.uk/genuki/Transcriptions/NBL/MWOO.html

Nottinghamshire

Civil Registration

- Registration Districts in Nottinghamshire
  www.fhsc.org.uk/genuki/REG/ntt.htm
  Betwen 1837 and 1930

Parish & Non-Parochial registers: Introductory Pages & Lists

- Nottinghamshire Family History Society: Parish Register List for Searching
  www.nottsfhs.org.uk
  Click on 'Research' and 'Parishes Searched'. List of transcripts held.
- Nottinghamshire
  www.sog.org.uk/prc/nottinghamshire.html
  Parish registers, printed, typescript, *etc.,* in the library of the Society of Genealogists
- Quaker Family History Society: Nottinghamshire
  www.rootsweb.com/~engqfhs/Research/counties/notts.htm
  Notes on Quaker records

Indexes

- Nottinghamshire Records Search
  www.genogold.com/notts/notts_search.php
  Parish register database; includes Bingham, Bleasby, Blidworth, Bunny, Eakring, East Bridgford, East Stoke, Farndon, Gonalston, Lenton, Lowdham, Rolleston, Sneinton, & Southwell at present
- National Burial Index (Nottinghamshire F.H.S.)
  www.familyhistoryonline.co.uk/database/NBINottsFHS.shtml
  Pay per view
- National Burial Index (Mansfield and District F.H.S.)
  www.familyhistoryonline.co.uk/database/NBIMansfieldDFHS.shtml
  Pay per view
- IGI Batch Numbers for Nottingham, England
  freepages.genealogy.rootsweb.com/~hughwallis/IGIBatchNumbers/CountyNottingham.htm

- Nottinghamshire, England: Parish and Probate Indexes
  www.ancestry.com/search/db.aspx?dbid=5917
  Index to published registers

Marriage Licences

- Nottinghamshire Marriage Licences
  homepages.nildram.co.uk/~jimella/marlic01.htm
  For 1578-1604

- Nottinghamshire Marriage Licence Bonds
  freespace.virgin.net/guy/etchells/NML.htm
  1701 only available at present, but more in progress

Collections of Transcripts on the Web

- Nottinghamshire Church Register Transcriptions & Indexes
  www.neep.demon.co.uk/nottsreg/index.html
  List of on-line transcripts. This page has been removed from the web, but is archived at **www.waybackmachine.org**

- Nottinghamshire Stray Marriages
  homepages.nildram.co.uk/~jimella/strays01.htm
  Collection of web-pages, separately listed below, and including an index

- Selected Nottinghamshire Parish Registers
  homepages.nildram.co.uk/~jimella/preg01.htm
  Collection of web-pages, individually listed below, with separate index

Publications

- Nottinghamshire Family History Society: the Online Shop
  www.nottsfhs.org.uk/bookshop/system/index.html
  Includes parish registers *etc.* published by the society

Arnold

- Parish Register of Arnold Marriages
  homepage.ntlworld.com/tomals/parish_register_of_arnold_marria.htm
  From the published Phillimore transcription, 1546-1812

Beckingham

- Parish register transcriptions of Beckingham, Nottinghamshire, for the years 1634, 1637 & 1641
  homepages.nildram.co.uk/~jimella/beck01.htm

Bilborough

- Bilborough, Nottinghamshire: Marriages 1569-1812
  www.neep.demon.co.uk/fhist/notts/bilborough_marr1.html
  This page has been removed from the web, but is archived at **www.waybackmachine.org**

Bilsthorpe

- Nottinghamshire Stray Marriages in Bilsthorpe
  homepages.nildram.co.uk/~jimella/strays09.htm

Bingham

- Bingham Parish Records
  freespace.virgin.net/guy.etchells/Bnprindex.htm
  Marriages, 1598-1812

Bleasby

- Parish Register Transcripts of Bleasby, Nottinghamshire for the Year 1633
  homepages.nildram.co.uk/~jimella/bleas01.htm

Blidworth

- Parish Register Transcripts of Blidworth, Nottinghamshire for the Year 1638
  homepages.nildram.co.uk/~jimella/blid01.htm

Bunny

- Bunny Village
  www.bunnyvillage.org.uk
  Includes baptisms 1715-1812, marriages 1556-1818, & burials 1715-1899

Calverton

- Parish Register Transcripts of Calverton, Nottinghamshire for the Years 1617 & 1623
  homepages.nildram.co.uk/~jimella/calvpr01.htm

- Nottinghamshire Stray Marriages in Calverton
  homepages.nildram.co.uk/~jimella/strays04.htm

Cropwell Bishop
- Parish Register Transcripts of Cropwell Bishop, Nottinghamshire for the Years 1638 & 1641
  homepages.nildram.co.uk/~jimella/crpbish1.htm

Darlton
- Parish Register Transcripts of Darlton, Nottinghamshire for the Years 1622, 1633 & 1641
  homepages.nildram.co.uk/~jimella/darl01.htm

Dunham
- Parish Register Transcripts of Dunham, Nottinghamshire for the Year 1641
  homepages.nildram.co.uk/~jimella/dun01.htm

Eakring
- Nottinghamshire Stray Marriages in Eakring
  homepages.nildram.co.uk/~jimella/strays30.htm

Edingley
- Parish Register Transcripts of Edingley, Nottinghamshire for the Year 1638
  homepages.nildram.co.uk/~jimella/eding01.htm

Elston
- Elston Chapel Marriages (1584-1721)
  freespace.virgin.net/guy.etchells/ECM1.htm
  Continued to 1814 at **/ECM2.htm**
- Elston Village Marriages (1573-1716)
  freespace.virgin.net/guy.etchells/EVM1.htm
  Continued as follows:
  1717-51 **/EVM2.htm** 1751-1811 **/EVM3.htm**

Elton on the Hill
- Elton-on-the-Hill Parish Records
  freespace.virgin.net/guy.etchells/Eltprindex.htm
  Marriages, 1593-1812

Farnsfield
- Parish Register Transcripts of Farnsfield, Nottinghamshire for the Year 1623
  homepages.nildram.co.uk/~jimella/farnsfd1.htm

Halam
- Parish Register Transcripts of Halam, Nottinghamshire for the Years 1622 & 1637
  homepages.nildram.co.uk/~jimella/halam1.htm

Halloughton
- Parish Register Transcripts of Halloughton, Nottinghamshire for the Years 1622, 1633 & 1641
  homepages.nildram.co.uk/~jimella/hall01.htm

Hickling
- Hickling Parish Records
  freespace.genealogy.rootsweb.com/~framland/par/Hiprindex.htm
  Marriages 1646-1812

Holme
- Parish Register Transcripts of Holme, Nottinghamshire for the Years 1623, 1625, 1628, 1638 & 1641
  homepages.nildram.co.uk/~jimella/holme1.htm

Kirklington
- Parish Register Transcripts of Kirklington, Nottinghamshire for the Years 1622 & 1638
  homepages.nildram.co.uk/~jimella/kirk1.htm

Lambley
- Nottinghamshire Stray Marriages in Lambley
  homepages.nildram.co.uk/~jimella/strays07.htm

Lenton
- Lenton Parish & Priory Records
  freespace.virgin.net/guy.etchells/Lenprindex.htm
  Selected abstracts of Lenton Register, 1540-1848

Little Carlton
- Little Carlton Transcriptions
  www.wparkinson.com/Little%20Carlton.htm
  Baptisms 1813-1978; marriages 1813-37

Mansfield

- Index of Mansfield Entries in local Quaker Registers to 1837, with additional information on Sufferings to 1798
  www.ukonline.co.uk/lost-mansfield/lmmisc/quaker1.htm

Morton

- Parish Register Transcripts of Morton, Nottinghamshire for the Years 1622 & 1623
  homepages.nildram.co.uk/~jimella/morton1.html

Newark

- Church Register Transcriptions, Newark, Nottinghamshire
  freepages.genealogy.rootsweb.com/~parishregisters/nottinghamshire/newark/newark.htm
  Also available at
  www.parishregisters.co.uk
  (click on 'Nottinghamshire' and 'Newark'). Includes St. Leonards baptisms 1873-5, and St. Mary burials 1811-12.

North Muskham

- Parish Register Transcripts of North Muskham, Nottinghamshire, for the Years 1623, 1633 & 1638
  homepages.nildram.co.uk/~jimella/nmusk1.htm

Norton Cuckney

- Norton Cuckney Parish Records
  freepages.genealogy.rootsweb.com/~brianjohnson/Cuckney/Records.htm
  Extracts from baptisms 1700-1900, marriages 1700-1899, & burials 1715-1847

Norwell

- Parish Register Transcripts of Norwell, Nottinghamshire for the Years 1638 & 1641
  homepages.nildram.co.uk/~jimella/norwell1.htm

Nottingham

- Nottingham Cemeteries
  www.genuki.org.uk/big/eng/NTT/Nottingham/Cemeteries.html
  Introductory notes

Oxton

- Parish Register Transcripts of Oxton, Nottinghamshire, for the Year 1622
  homepages.nildram.co.uk/~jimella/oxtonpr1.htm

- Nottinghamshire Stray Marriages in Oxton
  homepages.nildram.co.uk/~jimella/strays06.htm

Ragnall

- Parish Register Transcripts of Ragnall, Nottinghamshire, for the Year 1623
  homepages.nildram.co.uk/~jimella/ragnall1.htm

South Muskham

- Parish Register Transcripts of South Muskham, Nottinghamshire for the Year 1623
  homepages.nildram.co.uk/~jimella/smusk1.htm

Southwell

- Parish Register Transcripts of Southwell, Nottinghamshire for the Years 1633 & 1641
  homepages.nildram.co.uk/~jimella/sthwll1.htm

Strelley

- Strelley, Nottinghamshire: Marriages 1665-1812
  www.neep.demon.co.uk/fhist/notts/strelley_marriages1.html
  This page has been removed from the web, but is archived at
  www.waybackmachine.org

Sutton in Ashfield

- Parliament Street Chapel & Burial Ground: some burials between 1775 & 1797
  www.genealogy-links.co.uk/html/ash.burials.html
  In Sutton in Ashfield

Thurgaton

- Nottinghamshire Stray Marriages in Thurgaton
  homepages.nildram.co.uk/~jimella/strays05.htm

Tythby

- Parish Register Transcripts of Tithby, Nottinghamshire, for the Year 1625
  homepages.nildram.co.uk/~jimella/tithby1.htm

- Nottinghamshire Stray Marriages in Tithby
  homepages.nildram.co.uk/~jimella/strays08.htm

Upton
- Parish Register Transcripts of Upton, Nottinghamshire, for the Years 1633 & 1638
  homepages.nildram.co.uk/~jimella/upton01.htm

Wollaton
- Baptisms at Wollaton St. Leonards 1732-1800
  www.genuki.org.uk/big/eng/Notts/Transcriptions/wollbap1.txt

Woodborough
- Parish Register Transcripts of Woodborough, Nottinghamshire, for the Years 1623, 1627, 1637, 1638 & 1640
  homepages.nildram.co.uk/~jimella/woodbr01.htm

Rutland

Civil Registration
- Registration Districts in Rutland
  www.fhsc.org.uk/genuki/REG/rut.htm
  Between 1837 and 1930

Parish & Non-Parochial Registers: Introductory Pages & Lists
- Rutland
  www.sog.org.uk/prc/rutland.html
  Parish registers, printed, typescript, *etc.,* in the library of the Society of Genealogists

Indexes
- IGI Batch Numbers for Rutland, England
  freepages.genealogy.rootsweb.com/~hughwallis/IGIBatchNumbers/CountyRutland.htm

- Rutland, England: Parish and Probate Records
  www.ancestry.com/search/dbaspx?dbid=5928
  Index to published registers

North Luffenham
- [Marriages at North Luffenham, 1565-1812]
  www.uk-genealogy.org.uk/datafiles/marriagesearch.html
  Search 'North Luffenham'

Staffordshire

Civil Registration

- Registration Districts in Staffordshire
  www.fhsc.org.uk/genuki/REG/sts.htm
  Between 1837 and 1930
- Staffordshire Registration Service
  www.staffordshire.gov.uk/registration/
- Registration Service
  www.wolverhampton.gov.uk/community_living/life_events/registration/default.htm
  At Wolverhampton
- Staffordshire BMD
  web1.netnation.com/~bmsgh/staffsbmd/
  Index to civil registers held by district registrars
- West Midlands BMD: Births, Marriages and Deaths on the Internet
  www.bmsgh.org.uk/wmbmd/index.html
  Index to civil registers held by district registrars, covering the southern part of Staffordshire as well as parts of Warwickshire and Worcestershire
- Walsall Local History Centre
  www.walsall.gov.uk/localhistorycentre/
  Click on 'local churches' for list of parish registers held
- [St. Catherine's House Marriage Index, Jan-March, 1849. District 17. Staffordshire]
  www.cs.ncl.ac.uk/genuki/StCathsTranscriptions/CATH4917.TXT

Parish & Non-Parochial Registers: Introductory Pages & Lists
See also Warwickshire

- Staffordshire Church Records: Location, Guides & Indexes
  www.genuki.org.uk/big/eng/STS/ChurchRecords.html
- A Guide to Church of England Parish Registers
  www.wolverhamptonarchives.dial.pipex.com/pdf.files/coeregs.pdf
  At Wolverhampton Archives & Local Studies
- Nonconformist Registers & Roman Catholic Registers
  www.wolverhamptonarchives.dial.pipex.com/pdf.files/noncregs.pdf
  At Wolverhampton Archives & Local Studies
- Staffordshire
  www.sog.org.uk/prc/staffordshire.html
  Parish registers, printed, typescript, *etc.,* in the library of the Society of Genealogists
- Quaker Family History Society: Staffordshire
  www.rootsweb.com/~engqfhs/Research/counties/staffs.htm
  Notes on Quaker records

Indexes

- Staffordshire Marriages or Banns
  www.familyhistoryonline.co.uk/database/BMSGHSTSMar.shtml
  Pay per view
- Staffordshire Burials
  www.familyhistoryonline.co.uk/database/BMSGHSTSbur.shtml
  Pay per view
- National Burial Index (Birmingham & Midland S.G.H.)
  www.familyhistoryonline.co.uk/database/NBIBMSGH.shtml
  Pay per view
- B.M.S.G.H. Search Services
  www.bmsgh.org/search/sea1.html
  Details of various marriage and burial indexes *etc.,* for Staffordshire, Warwickshire and Worcestershire
- Free Reg: Staffordshire
  freereg.rootsweb.com/parishes/sts/index.htm
  Details of the registers currently included in a project to index births, marriages and deaths
- Privately Owned Indexes Relating to Staffordshire, Warwickshire or Worcestershire
  www.bmsgh.org/search/sea4.html
  Lists various indexes to parish registers *etc.*
- Staffordshire Parishes in the British Vital Records Index (VRI)
  www.genuki.org.uk/big/eng/STS/VRI2.html

- IGI Batch Numbers for Stafford, England
  freepages.genealogy.rootsweb.com/~hughwallis/IGIBatchNumbers/CountyStafford_(A-M).htm
  Continued at **/CountyStafford_(N-Z).htm**

- Staffordshire, England: Parish and Probate Records
  www.ancestry.com/search/db.aspx?dbid=5934
  Index to published registers

Transcript Collections on the Web

- Church of England Parish Registers
  www.wolverhamptonarchives.dial.pipex.com/par-registers.htm
  Collection of online indexes on the Wolverhampton Archives site. Individual pages listed below separately

- Transcriptions from Staffordshire Records
  uk-transcriptions.accessgenealogy.com/Staffs.htm

- Transcripts of Nonconformist Registers
  www.wolverhamptonarchives.dial.pipex.com/noncon-regs.htm
  Collection of transcripts on the Wolverhampton Archives site, separately listed here.

Publications

- B.M.S.G.H. Bookshop: Staffordshire: Parishes, Census Districts & Other Places
  www.bmsgh.org/bookshop/staffs/sta.html
  Lists parish registers and monumental inscriptions available in fiche and book formats

- Staffordshire Parish Register Society
  www.sprs.org.uk
  Includes list of registers published by the Society

Berkswich

- Parish of Berkswich: the Parish Registers
  www.berkswich.org.uk/
  Click on 'genealogies page' and 'Parish registers'. Includes baptisms 1601-1906, marriages 1601-1905, & burials 1601-1963

- Berkswich Parish Registers, 1613-1821
  uk-transcriptions.accessgenealogy.com/Berkswich%20PR.htm

Betley

- Betley Parish Registers 1538-1812
  www.jcorness.fsnet.co.uk/parish%20registers/Registers%20frame.htm
  From the edition published in 1916

Bilston

- Bilston: St. Leonard's Church Registers: Registers of Baptisms 1686-1812, Marriages 1686-1754 and Burials 1727-1812
  www.wolverhamptonarchives.dial.pipex.com/stleonard.htm
  Surname index

- Bilston High Street Primitive Methodist Church transcripts of church registers
  www.gpt63.dial.pipex.com/non-con/bil-highst.pdf
  Baptisms 1827-37

- Swan Bank Wesleyan Methodist Church: Transcripts of Church Registers
  www.gpt63.dial.pipex.com/non-con/swanbank-baps.pdf
  www.wolverhamptonarchives.dial.pipex.com/pdf.files/non-con/swanbank-baps.pdf
  Index to Bilston baptisms, 1816-1838 at Bilston

- Oxford Street Independent Chapel: transcripts of Church Registers
  www.wolverhamptonarchives.dial.pipex.com/pdf/files/non-con/oxf-st.pdf
  Index of baptisms, 1786-1837

- Bilston: Swan Bank Methodist: Burials 1823-1837
  www.wolverhamptonarchives.dial.pipex.com/swanb-bur.htm
  Index

- Authentic List of the Victims of the First Asiatic Cholera Visitation in the Bilston Parish in 1832
  www.gpt63.dial.pipex.com/bilston/cholera.pdf

Blackheath

- St. Paul's, Blackheath Baptisms, Marriages and Burials
  uk-transcriptions.accessgenealogy.com/St.Paul's,Blackheath.htm
  Covers 1870-1929

Blakenhall

- St. Luke's, Blakenhall, Wolverhampton, Marriages 1895-1929
  uk-transcriptions.accessgenealogy.com/
  St.Luke's,Blakenhall%20Marriages.htm

Burton on Trent

- Burton on Trent General Baptist Births
  freepages.genealogy.rootsweb.com/~blanchec/BurtTbirth.htm
  For the 1820's & 1830's

Caverswall

- Caverswall Parish Registers
  www.caverswall.org.uk/sprs_surname_index.htm
  List of surnames in the published registers

Cradley Heath

- St. Luke's, Cradley Heath Marriages
  uk-transcriptions.accessgenealogy.com/
  St.Luke's,Cradley%20Heath.htm
  Covers 1849-1897. Also includes baptisms 1847-1901 & burials 1850-1967

Darlaston

- Register of St. Lawrence, Darlaston, Staffordshire 1544 to 1599
  familyties.homestead.com/files/StLawrence/
  1544_1599_BMD_St_Law_Darl.pdf
  Continued as follows:
  1600-1635 **/St.Lawrence,Darlaston%201600-1635.htm**
  1636-1664 **/St.Lawrence,Darlaston%201636-1664.htm**
  1665-1692 **/St.Lawrence,Darlaston%201665-1692.htm**

Gnosall

- Gnosall Parish Registers (Marriages) 1572-1785
  www.geocities.brigaban/gnosallpr13.html

Handsworth

- Digital Handsworth: Baptismal Register
  www.search.digitalhandsworth.org.uk/
  Click on 'search' and 'keyword', and search 'baptismal'. Facsimile of original register, 1870-90

Hints

- A Record of Baptisms, Marriages and Burials at Hints
  www.hints-village.com/
  Click on title. Baptisms 1559-1812, marriages 1558-1812, & burials 1680-1812

Kingswinford

- St. Mary's, Kingswinford Marriages & Baptisms (Partial Transcription)
  uk-transcriptions.accessgenealogy.com/St.Mary's,Kingswinford.htm
  Covers 1838-1864

Knutton

- Knutton, Staffordshire, Baptisms, Burials & Marriages
  uk-transcriptions.accessgenealogy.com/Knutton.htm
  19-20th c.

Leek

- Parish Registers at Leek Library (on microfilm)
  homepage.ntlworld.com/billharrison/gene.html
  Click on 'genealogical sources' and title

Newcastle under Lyme

- St. Gile's, Newcastle Births & Marriages (Various)
  uk-transcriptions.accessgenealogy.com/St.Gile's.htm
  1777-1811. Incomplete?

Old Hill

- Holy Trinity, Old Hill Baptisms & Marriages
  uk-transcriptions.accessgenealogy.com/Holy%20Trinity.htm
  Covers 1876-1908. Continued to 1920 at
  /Holy%Trinity%20Baptisms.htm

- Tabernacle, Old Hill Baptisms & Marriages (Partial)
  uk-transcriptions.accessgenealogy.com/Tabernacle,Old%20Hill.htm
  Covers 1909-1958

Rowley Regis

- St. Gile's, Rowley Regis Baptisms, Marriages & Burials
  uk-transcriptions.accessgenealogy.com/St.Gile's,Rowley%20Regis.htm
  18-19th c.

- Extracts from the Burial Register of Rowley Regis, Staffordshire
  privatewww.essex.ac.uk/~alan/articles/Rowley.html
  Brief extracts, 1794-1812

Sedgley

- Extracts from the Sedgley Parish Registers
  www.sedgleymanor.com/registers/registers_front.html
  Covers 1558-1601

Silverdale

- St. Luke's, Silverdale, Staffordshire Births, Burials & Marriages
  uk-transcriptions.accessgenealogy.com/Silverdale.htm
  Covers 1879-1931

Snow Hill

- Snow Hill Unitarian Chapel transcripts of church registers
  www.gpt63.dial.pipex.com/non-con/snow-hill-baps.pdf
  Index of Baptisms 1830-37

Swynnerton

- St. Mary's Church, Swynnerton: Church Records
  www.btinternet.com/~st.marys/
  Click on 'features' and 'church records'. Covers 1558-1711.

Walsall

- Deaths & Memoriams, *Walsall Observer,* 23 Jan 1932
  uk-transcriptions.accessgenealogy.com/Walsall%20Observer%20Deaths.htm

Wednesbury

- Wednesbury, St. John: Burials
  www.genuki.org.uk/big/eng/STS/Wednesbury/StJohn/BurialsAC.html
  Index, late 19th c. Continued on 3 further pages

Wednesfield

- Wednesfield: St. Thomas's Church Registers: Registers of Baptisms 1751-1837 and burials 1751-1837
  www.wolverhamptonarchives.dial.pipex.com/stthomas_index1.htm
  Surname index

West Bromwich

- [All Saints West Bromwich: Marriages 1658-1754 & 1795-1837]
  familyties6.homestead.com/AllSaintsMarriages.html
  Continued to 1837 on 16 further pages. For index, see
  www.geocities.com/ann_margetson/allsaintswb.htm

Willenhall

- Willenhall: St. Giles' Church Registers: Registers of Baptisms 1642-1812 and Burials 1727-1812
  www.wolverhamptonarchives.dial.pipex.com/stgiles.htm
  Surname index

- Transcript of entries from St. Giles, Willenhall, Parish Registers
  freespace.virgin.net/willen.hall/ah/transcripts.html
  Pages of extracts for 15 different families

Wolverhampton

- Darlington Street Methodist Church: transcripts of Church Registers
  www.gpt63.dial.pipex.com/non-con/darlington-st.pdf
  Index of baptisms, 1793-1837

- George Street Methodist Church transcripts of church registers
  www.gpt63.dial.pipex.com/non-con/george-st.pdf
  Index of baptisms 1825-37

- John Street Presbyterian Chapel Transcripts of Church Registers
  www.gpt63.dial.pipex.com/non-con/john-st-bap.pdf
  Index of baptisms, 1727-1815. For burials, 1726-9, see
  /john-st-bur.pdf

- Queen Street Independent Chapel Transcripts of Church Registers
  www.gpt63.dial.pipex.com/non-con/queen-st.pdf
  Baptisms 1785-1836

- Temple Street Independent Chapel Transcripts of Church Registers
  www.gpt63.dial.pipex.com.non-con/temple-st-baps.htm
  Index of baptisms 1772-1836. For burials 1784-99, see
  /temple-st-burs.pdf

- Wolverhampton: St. Peter's Church Registers: Registers of Baptisms 1539-1812, Marriages 1539-1838, and Burials 1539-1812
  www.wolverhamptonarchives.dial.pipex.com/stpeter_index1.htm
  Surname index

- St. James', Wolverhamptons Baptisms & Marriages
  uk-transcriptions.accessgenealogy.com/St.James,Wolverhampton.htm
  Covers 1860-1930

- Walsall Street Baptist Chapel Transcripts of Church Registers
  www.gpt63.dial.pipex.com/non-con/walsall-st-baps.pdf
  Index of baptisms 1832-7

Suffolk

Civil Registration

- Registration Districts of Suffolk in 1836, with Maps and List of Parishes
  www.jhoddy.demon.co.uk/murrels/index.htm

- Registration Districts in Suffolk
  www.fhsc.org.uk/genuki/REG/sfk.htm
  Between 1837 and 1930

Parish & Non-Parochial Registers: Introductory Pages & Lists

- Suffolk
  www.sog.org.uk/prc/suffolk.html
  Parish registers, printed, typescript, *etc.,* in the library of the Society of Genealogists

- Quaker Family History Society: Suffolk
  www.rootsweb.com/engqfhs/Research/counties/suffolk.htm
  Notes on Quaker records

Indexes

- Suffolk Baptism Index
  www.familyhistoryonline.co.uk/database/SFKBaptismIndex.shtml
  Pay per view

- Suffolk Marriage Index
  www.familyhistoryonline.co.uk/database/SFKMarriageIndex.shtml
  Pay per view

- Suffolk Marriage Index (1813-37)
  www.familyhistoryonline.co.uk/database/SFKMarr1813.shtml
  Pay per view

- National Burial Index (Suffolk Family History Society)
  www.familyhistoryonline.co.uk/database/NBISuffolkFHS.shtml
  Pay per view

- Suffolk 'Early' Burial Index
  www.familyhistoryonline.co.uk/database/SFKBurialIndex.shtml
  Pay per view. Primarily, but not wholly, from earlier registers

- National Burial Index (Felixstowe Family History Society)
  www.familyhistoryonline.co.uk/database/NBIFelixstoweFHS.shtml
  Pay per view
- Boyd's Marriage Index: Parishes and Period of Records: Suffolk
  www.britishorigins.com/help/popup-aboutbo-bmi-parish.htm
  Click on 'Suffolk'
- IGI Batch Numbers for Suffolk, England
  freepages.genealogy.rootsweb.com/~hughwallis/IGIBatchNumbers/CountySuffolk.htm
- Batches extracted from Bishops' Transcripts for the whole County of Suffolk
  freepages.genealogy.rootsweb.com/~hughwallis/IGISpecialBatches.htm#Suffolk
- A Selection of Military Marriages, Indexed from Newspapers and Books. Mainly covering Suffolk with a few other counties and countries
  homepages.rootsweb.com/~mwi/milmarr.txt

Publications

- Parish Registers available for Purchase in Microform
  www.suffolkcc.gov.uk/sro/parishlist.html
  From Suffolk Record Office
- Suffolk Family History Society: Suffolk Marriage Index
  www.suffolkfhs.co.uk/marry.html
  Details of a series of booklets/fiche covering 1813-37
- The Family History Shop
  www.jenlibrary.u-net.com/
  Many transcripts of parish registers for Suffolk, Norfolk and Cornwall for sale
- Suffolk Family History Society: Suffolk Marriage Index
  www.suffolkfhs.co.uk/marry.html
  Details of a series of booklets/fiche covering 1813-37

Transcript Collections on the Web

- Suffolk Parish Registers Index
  www.rootsweb.com/~engdorse/PRSU.html
  Collection of pages with contributed extracts only
- The Cemeteries Index
  www.waveney.gov.uk/cemetery/cemeteries.htm
  For Waveney District; pages for individual places are separately listed here
- The Cosford Database
  www.cosford-database.co.uk
  Details of over 80,000 people mainly from the Cosford and Lavenham Registration Districts, and including births marriages and deaths. Pages for particular parishes are listed separately here

Acton

- Acton, Suffolk
  fp.raylong.plus.com/acton/index.htm
  Brief pedigrees based on the registers

Aldham

- Aldham, Suffolk
  fp.raylong.plus.com/oldham/index.html
  Brief pedigrees based on the registers

Beccles

- Beccles Cemetery Index
  www.waveney.gov.uk/cemetery/beccles/beccles.html
  Register index, 20-21st c.
- *Beccles and Bungay News*
  www.genuki.org.uk/big/eng/SFK/BecclesandBungay/
  Primarily transcripts of birth, marriage, and death entries in the *Beccles and Bungay Weekly News,* 1858-69

Belle Vue Park

- Belle Vue Park Cemetery Index
  www.waveney.gov.uk/cemetery/belle_vue_park/belle_vue_park.html
  Register index, 20-21st c.

Bildeston

- Bildeston, Suffolk
  fp.raylong.plus.com/bilder/index.html
  Brief pedigrees based on the registers

Boxford

- Boxford, Suffolk
  fp.raylong.plus.com/boxford/index.html
  Brief pedigrees based on the registers

Brent Eleigh

- Brent Eleigh, Suffolk
  fp.raylong.plus.com/beleigh/index.html
  Brief pedigrees based on the registers

Brettenham

- Brettenham, Suffolk
  fp.raylong.plus.com/brett/index.html
  Brief pedigrees based on the registers

Bungay

See also Beccles

- The Bungay Cemetery Index
  www.waveney.gov.uk/cemetery/bungay/bungay.html
  Register index, late 19th-2oth c.

Chedburgh

- Suffolk Parish Registers Index: Chedburgh Baptisms 1800-1850
  www.rootsweb.com/~engdorse/Suffolk/Chedburgh.B.html
  Contributed entries. Brief

Chelsworth

- Chelsworth, Suffolk
  fp.raylong.plus.com/chels/index.html
  Brief pedigrees based on the registers

Chevington

- Suffolk Parish Registers Index: Chevington Baptisms 1700-1880
  www.rootsweb.com/~engdorse/Suffolk/Chevington/B.html
  Contributed entries only

- Suffolk Parish Registers Index: Chevington Parish Burials 1700-1900
  www.rootsweb.com/~engdorse/Suffolk/Chevington/D.html
  Contributed entries only

Cockfield

- Cockfield, Suffolk
  fp.raylong.plus.com/cfield/index.html
  Brief pedigrees based on the registers

Earl Stonham

- Suffolk Parish Registers Index: Earl Stonham Baptisms 1654-1690
  www.rootsweb.com/~engdorse/EARL-STONHAM.html
  Continued to 1850 on 4 further pages. Contributed entries only

Edwardstone

- Edwardstone, Suffolk
  fp.raylong.plus.com/edward/index.html
  Brief pedigrees based on the registers

Elmsett

- Elmsett, Suffolk
  fp.raylong.plus.com/elmsett/index.html
  Brief pedigrees based on the registers

Great Waldingfield

- Great Waldingfield, Suffolk
  fp.raylong.plus.com/gtw/index.html
  Brief pedigrees based on the registers

Groton

- Groton, Suffolk
  fp.raylong.plus.com/groton/index.html
  Brief pedigrees based on the registers

Hadleigh

- Hadleigh, Suffolk
  fp.raylong.plus.com/hadleigh/index.html
  Brief pedigrees based on the registers

Hadleigh Hamlet

- Hadleigh Hamlet, Suffolk
  fp.raylong.plus.com/hhamlet/index.html
  Brief pedigrees based on the registers

Halesworth

- The Halesworth Cemetery Index
  www.waveney.gov.uk/cemetery/halesworth/halesworth.html
  Register index, late 19th-20th c.

Haverhill

- Haverhill Independant Baptisms
  www.haverhill-uk.com/genealogy/baptisms/haverhill__baptisms.shtml
  Covers 1881-5
- Haverhill Old Independant Marriages
  www.haverhill-uk.com/genealogy/marriages/haverhill__independant__church__marriages.shtml
  Covers 1899-1902
- Haverhill Cemetery Burial Records
  www.haverhill-uk.com/genealogy/cemetery/index.shtml
  Database, 1867-1950

Hundon

- Hundon Church Baptisms 1674-1837
  www.haverhill-uk.com/genealogy.baptisms/hundon__baptisms1.shtml
  Continued to 1913 at **/hundon__baptisms2.shtml**
- Hundon Church Banns 1837 to 1913
  www.haverhill-uk.com/genealogy/marriages/hundon__church__banns.shtml
- Hundon Church Marriages 1674 to 1837
  www.haverhill-uk.com/genealogy/marriages/hundon__church__marriages1.shtml
  Continued to 1910 at **/hundon__church__marriages2.html**
- Hundon Church Burials 1674 to 1836
  www.haverhill-uk.com/genealogy/burials/hundon__church__burials1.shtml
  Continued to 1900 at **/hundon__church__burials2.shtml**
- Hundon Chapel Marriages
  www.haverhill-uk.com/genealogy/marriages/hundon__chapel__marriages.shtml
  1883-1904
- Hundon Chapel Burials
  www.haverhill-uk.com/genealogy/burials/hundon__chapel__burials.shtml
  1882-1909

Kersey

- Kersey, Suffolk
  fp.raylong.plus.com/kersey/index.html
  Brief pedigrees based on the registers

Kettlebaston

- Kettlebaston, Suffolk
  fp.raylong.plus.com/kettle/index.html
  Brief pedigrees based on the registers

Kirkley

- Kirkley Cemetery Index
  www.waveney.gov.uk/cemetery/kirkley/kirkley__abbot__boggis.html
  Register index, late 19th-20th c.

Lavenham

- Lavenham, Suffolk
  fp.raylong.plus.com/lavenham/index.html
  Brief pedigrees based on the registers

Lawshall

- Lawshall, Suffolk
  fp.raylong.plus.com/lawshall/index.html
  Brief pedigrees based on the registers

Layham

- Layham, Suffolk
  fp.raylong.plus.com/layham/index.html
  Brief pedigrees based on the registers

Lindsey

- Lindsey, Suffolk
  fp.raylong.plus.com/lindsey/index.html
  Brief pedigrees based on the registers

Little Saxham

- Little Saxham Parish Registers
  www.little-saxham.suffolk.gov.uk/history/registers.shtml
  In progress

Long Melford

- Long Melford, Suffolk
  fp.raylong.plus.com/melford/index.html
  Brief pedigrees based on the registers

- Long Melford, Suffolk: details taken from the Long Melford Parish Magazine, October 1882
  thor.prohosting.com/~hughes/Lmelford.txt
  Includes extracts from parish registers

Lowestoft

- Lowestoft Cemetery Index
  www.waveney.gov.uk/cemetery/lowestoft/lowestoft__abott__barbor.html
  Register index, late 19th-20th c.

- Index of Surnames: Baptisms 1841-53
  www.genuki.org.uk/big/eng/SFK/LowestoftStMargarets/LowestoftStMChr.txt
  At St. Margaret's, Lowestoft

- Index of Surnames: Burials 1745-1812
  www.genuki.org.uk/big/eng/SFK/LowestoftSt.Margarets/LowestoftStMBu.txt
  At St. Margaret's, Lowestoft

Milden

- Milden, Suffolk
  fp.raylong.plus.com/milden/index.html
  Brief pedigrees based on the registers

Monks Eleigh

- Monks Eleigh, Suffolk
  fp.raylong.plus.com/meleigh/index.html
  Brief pedigrees based on the registers

Monks Soham

- Index of Marriages for Monks Soham 1712-1918
  www.genuki.org.uk/big/eng/SFK/MonkSoham/MonkSohamMR.txt

Naughton

- Naughton, Suffolk
  fp.raylong.plus.com/naughton/index.html
  Brief pedigrees based on the registers

Nedging

- Nedging, Suffolk
  fp.raylong.plus.com/nedging/index.html
  Brief pedigrees based on the registers

Orford

- Transcript of the Parish Register of Orford, Suffolk: Burials 1538-1630
  www.newenglandancestors.org/research/database/orford/default.asp
  Searchable database

Preston

- Preston Parish Records
  www.prestonstmary.co.uk/ParishRecords.htm
  Indexes to baptisms from 1628, banns 1786-93 & 1824-1900, marriages 1628-1903 & burials from 1628

- Preston St. Mary, Suffolk
  fp.raylong.plus.com/preston/index.html
  Brief pedigrees based on the registers

Semer

- Semer, Suffolk
  fp.raylong.plus.com/semer/index.html
  Brief pedigrees based on the registers

Southwold

- Southwold Cemetery Index
  www.waveney.gov.uk/cemetery/southwold/southwold.html
  Register index, late 19-20th c.

Stowmarket

- Stowmarket, Suffolk
  fp.raylong.plus.com/stow/index.html
  Brief pedigrees based on the registers

Sudbury

- Sudbury St. Peter: Index of Brides and Grooms
  www.genuki.org.uk/big/eng/SFK/SudburyStPeters/SudburyStPMar.txt
  Index to a printed transcript

Thornham Magna

- Suffolk Parish Registers Index: Thornham Magna Baptisms 1555-1600
  www.rootsweb.com/~engdorse/Thornham_Magna.html
  Contributed entries only. Continued as follows:
  1601-1650 **/ThornhamMagna1.html**
  1651-1700 **/ThornhamMagna2.html**

Thorpe Morieux

- Thorpe Morieux, Suffolk
  fp.raylong.plus.com/thorpe/index.html
  Brief pedigrees based on the registers

Wattisham

- Wattisham, Suffolk
  fp.raylong.plus.com/wattish/index.html
  Brief pedigrees based on the registers

West Stow

- Index of the Parish Registers of West Stow, Suffolk
  homepages.rootsweb.com/~mwi/sfkwstprtxt
  Index entries from a printed edition, to 1850

Whatfield

- Whatfield, Suffolk
  fp.raylong.plus.com/whatf/index.html
  Brief pedigrees based on the registers

Wickham Skeith

- [Wickham Skeith Baptism Index 1685-1812]
  www.genuki.org.uk/big/eng/SFK/WickhamSkeith/ws_bap2.txt
  Continued to 1900 at **/ws_bap1.txt**

- [Wickham Skeith Marriage Index, 1685-1812]
  www.genuki.org.uk/big/eng/SFK/WickhamSkeith/ws_mar2.txt
  Continued to 1900 at **/ws_mar1.txt**

- [Wickham Skeith Burial Index 1685-1812]
  www.genuki.org.uk/big/eng/SFK/WickhamSkeith/ws_bur2.txt
  Continued to 1900 at **/ws_bur1.txt**

Woodbridge

- Beaumont Baptist Church Records
  www.btinternet.com/%7Ebeaumontbaptist/Records/
  At Woodbridge. Births/Baptisms, 1794-1896; marriages 1863-96; deaths 1793-1837 & 1862-95.

Woolpit

- Transcript of the Parish Register for Woolpit, Suffolk: Index to Baptisms Marriages and Burials
  www.pbenyon.plus.com/Den/Woolpit/Index.html
  freepages.genealogy.rootsweb.com/~pbtye/Den/Woolpit/Index.html

Worlington

- Parish Register Page
  www.sartorelli.gen.nz/parishregister.htm
  For Worlington. Baptisms 1721-79; marriages 1719-52; burials 1719-82

Wrentham

- Wrentham Cemetery Index
  www.waveney.gov.uk/cemetery/wrentham/wrentham.html
  Register index, 19-21st c.

Warwickshire

Civil Registration

- Registration Districts in Warwickshire
  www.fhsc.org.uk/genuki/REG/war.htm
  Between 1837 and 1930

- Registration Districts for Churches in the Following Areas
  www.genuki.org.uk/big/eng/WAR/birmingham/bregareas.html
  Covers Birmingham, Aston, Kings Norton, Solihull and West Bromwich Registration Districts.

Parish & Non-Parochial Registers: Introductory Pages & Lists

- Parish Registers held at Birmingham Central Library
  www.bham.de/index_churches.html
  Lists registers, transcripts, fiche, *etc.,* for Staffordshire, Warwickshire and Worcestershire. Does not list the substantial collections of published registers from other counties.

- Coventry & District Parish Registers: Parish Register Copies held at Coventry Archives
  www.covfhs.org.uk/
  Click on 'Research Aids' and 'Church Records'. List.

- Coventry Family History Society: Other Warwickshire Parish Registers: Warwickshire Parish Registers held at Coventry Archives
  www.covfhs.org.uk/
  Click on 'Research Aids' and 'Warwickshire P.R's'

- Coventry Non-Conformist Registers: Non-Conformist Registers held at Coventry Archives
  www.covfhs.org/
  Click on 'Research Aids' and 'Non-conformism'

- Parish Registers
  www.genuki.org.uk/big/eng/WAR/wcl/wclparish.html
  Brief list of registers held by Warwickshire County Library

- Parish Register Copies
  www.shakespeare.org.uk/main/3/90
  At Shakespeare Birthplace Trust

- Warwickshire
  www.sog.org.uk/prc/warwickshire.html
  Parish registers, printed, typescript, *etc.,* in the library of the Society of Genealogists

- Quaker Family History Society: Warwickshire
  www.rootsweb.com/~engqfhs/Research/counties/warks.htm
  Notes on Quaker records

Indexes

See also Staffordshire

- Greater Birmingham Marriage Index
  www.familyhistoryonline.co.uk/database/BMSGHBirmMar.shtml
  Pay per view

- Warwickshire Burials
  www.familyhistoryonline.co.uk/database/BMSGHWARbur.shtml
  Pay per view index

- National Burial Index (Birmingham & Midland S.G.H.)
  www.familyhistoryonline.co.uk/database/NBIBMSGH.shtml
  Pay per view; covers parts of Staffordshire, Warwickshire, and Worcestershire

- National Burial Index (Coventry F.H.S.)
  www.familyhistoryonline.co.uk/database/NBICoventryFHS.shtml
  Pay per view. Covers 15 parishes around Coventry

- National Burial Index (Nuneaton and N. Warwickshire F.H.S.)
  www.familyhistoryonline.co.uk/database/NBINuneatonNWFHS.shtml
  Pay per view

- IGI Batch Numbers for Warwick, England
  freepages.genealogy.rootsweb.com/~hughwallis/IGIBatchNumbers/CountyWarwick_(A-M).htm
  Continued at **/County Warwick_(N-Z).htm**

- Warwickshire, England: Parish and Probate Records
  www.ancestry.com/search/db.aspx?dbid=5942
  Index to published registers

Newspapers

- Extracts from Warwickshire Newspapers 1874-1907: Births
  www.hunimex.com/warwick/bmd/births_announcements_1874-1907.html

  See also:
  Marriages **/marriage_announcements_1874-1907.html**
  Deaths **/death_announcements_1874-1907.html**

Publications

- B.M.S.G.H. Bookshop: Warwickshire
  www.bmsgh.org/bookshop/warw/wa_a.html
  Lists parish registers *etc.,* in fiche and book formats
- Coventry Family History Society: Bookshop. Coventry & District Parish Registers
  www.covfhs.org.uk
  Click on 'Bookshop' and 'Parish Regs'
- Nuneaton and North Warwickshire Family History Society: Society Publications
  www.nnwfhs.org.uk/
  Click on 'Bookshop'. Includes some registers
- Rugby Family History Group: Microfiche
  www.rugbyfhs.co.uk
  Click on 'Microfiche'. Includes some parish registers
- The Warwickshire Family History Society: Publications
  www.wfhs.org.uk/html/information.html
  Includes some registers, *etc.*

Transcript Collections on the Web

- Pickards Pink Pages of Warwickshire Genealogy
  www.hunimex.com/warwick
  Collection of Warwickshire parish register pages, *etc.*

Atherstone

- Atherstone Baptisms 1875-1914
  www.hunimex.com/warwick/bmd/atherstone_bap_surnames.html
- Atherstone Marriages from 1899 to 1908
  www.hunimex.com/warwick/bmd/atherstone_marr_1899-1908.html
- Atherstone Burials from 1875 to 1902
  www.hunimex.com/warwick/bmd/atherstone_burials_1875-1902.html

Birmingham

- Parish Records, Birmingham Library
  www.genuki.org.uk/big/eng/WAR/deloyd/parishrecs.htm
  List of registers for Birmingham held
- Church Registers, Birmingham
  www.genuki.org.uk/big/eng/WAR/deloyd/nonconform.htm
  List of nonconformist and Roman Catholic registers
- [Birmingham BMD 1893]
  www.genuki.org.uk/big/eng/WAR/deloyd/Various1893.html
- Index to the Register of St. Martins, Birmingham 1653-1708, part 1
  www.genuki.org.uk/big/eng/WAR/deloyd/registerspart1.html
- St. Philips, Birmingham
  www.genuki.org.uk/big/eng/WAR/deloyd/stphilipmar.html
  Extracts from the marriage register, 1720-37
- Atherstone Burials from 1875 to 1902
  www.hunimex.com/warwick/bmd/atherstone_burials_1875-1902.html

Exhall

- Exhall and Wixford Marriages 1803 to 1836
  www.hunimex.com/warwick/Exhall_wixford_marr_1803-36.html

Foleshill

- Marriage Index for Foleshill, Warwickshire
  www.hunimex.com/warwick/foleshill_marriages_g.html
  Covers 1770-1911
- Foleshill St. Laurence Burials
  www.genuki.org.uk/big/eng/WAR/deloyd/Foleshillburials.html
  Surname index to 1843

Frankton

- Banns for Frankton, Warwickshire from 1824 to 1876
  www.hunimex.com/warwick/banns_frankton.html

Grandborough

- Banns for Grandborough, Warwickshire, from 1824 to 1894
  www.hunimex.com/warwick/banns_grandborough.html

Polesworth

- Burials for Polesworth, 1838-50
  www.hunimex.com/warwick/mi/polesworth_burials_1838-51.html

Stretton on Fosse

- Stretton-on-Fosse Links (Warwickshire, England)
  www.rootsweb.com/~engcots/Stretton.html
  Includes baptisms, marriages & burials strays 1538-1900

Wixhall

See Exhall

Westmorland

Civil Registration

See also Northumberland

- Registration Districts in Westmorland
  www.fhsc.org.uk/genuki/REG/wes.htm
  Between 1837 and 1930

Parish & Non-Parochial Registers: Introductory Pages & Lists

- Westmorland
  www.sog.org.uk/prc/westmorland.html
  Parish registers, printed, typescript, *etc.,* in the library of the Society of Genealogists

- Quaker Family History Society: Westmorland
  www.rootsweb.com/~engqfhs/Research/counties/west.htm
  Notes on Quaker records

Indexes

- IGI Batch Numbers for Westmorland, England
  freepages.genealogy.rootsweb.com/~hughwallis/IGIBatchNumbers/CountyWestmorland.htm
- Batch Numbers for Westmorland Churches
  www.genuki.org.uk/big/eng/WES/igi_batch_nos.htm

Transcript Collections on the Web

- Cumbria Genealogy Search: Transcripts Index
  edenlinks.rootsweb.com/1gp/RECORDS/TRANSINDEX.HTM

- Cumbrian Genealogy: Parish Registers (full listings)
  johnwatters.members.beeb.net/index.htm
  This page has been removed from the web, but is archived at **www.waybackmachine.org.uk**

Askham

- Askham Parish Registers
  edenlinks.rootsweb.com/1gp/RECORDS/ASKIND.HTM
  Covers 1566-1670, plus marriages and banns 1754-1812

Beetham

- Beetham Parish Registers
  edenlinks.rootsweb.com/beetham/INDEX_PAGE.HTM
  Covers 1690-1749

Cliburn

- Cumbrian Genealogy: Cliburn Parish Register 1565-1812
  johnwatters.members.beeb.net/CliburnAtoL.htm
  Index. Cntinued at **/CliburnMtoz.htm**. These pages have been removed from the web, but are archived at **www.waybackmachine.org**

Crosby Ravensworth

- Cumbrian Genealogy: Crosby Ravensworth; Births, Marriages & Deaths 1570-1812
  johnwatters.members.beeb.net/CrosRavA.htm
  Index. Continued on 13 further pages. These pages have been removed from the web, but are archived at **www.waybackmachine.org**

Kendal

- Cumbrian Genealogy: the Registers of Kendal
  johnwatters.members.beeb.net/Ken1558a.htm
  Covers 1558-87. Index continued on 2 further pages. These pages have been removed from the web, but are archived at **www.waybackmachine.org**

- Cumbrian Genealogy; Kendal Baptisms 1596-99, Marriages and Burials 1591-99 and Baptisms 1607-31
  johnwatters.members.beeb.net/Kendal3A.htm
  Continued on 14 further pages

Kirkby Stephen

- The Parish of Kirkby Stephen, Westmorland, England
  freepages.misc.rootsweb.com/~enzedders/index.htm
  Baptisms 1647-1730; marriages 1647-71 & 1676-1771; burials 1647-1773; Wesleyan burials 1843-1900, *etc.*

Kirkby Thore

- Cumbrian Genealogy Kirkby Thore Registers Miscellaneous Entries
  johnwatters.members.beeb.net/KyThore.html
  Parish register extracts, 1652-1724, originally published in the *Cumberland and Westmorland Antiquarian and Archaeological Society transactions* 1879. These pages have been removed from the web, but are archived at **www.waybackmachine.org**

Matterdale

- Matterdale Mart
  uk.msnusers.com/MartindaleMart
  Includes indexes of baptisms 1633-1748, marriages 1636-1881, & burials 1683-1904

- Matterdale Register Book 1: Burials 1634-1657
  edenlinks.rootsweb.com/1gp/RECORDS/MATTBUR1.HTM

Milburn

- Cumbrian Genealogy: Milburn Parish Register 1679-1812
  johnwatters.members.beeb.net/MilburnAtoG.htm
  Index, continued on 2 further pages. These pages have been removed from the web, but are archived at **www.waybackmachine.org**

Patterdale

- Patterdale Patter
  groups.msn.com/PatterdalePatter
  Includes indexes of baptisms 1763-1859, & burials 1763-1895

Yorkshire

Civil Registration

- Registration Districts in Yorkshire; East Riding
  www.fhsc.org.uk/genuki/REG/ery.htm
  Between 1837 and 1930

- Registration Districts in Yorkshire; North Riding
  www.fhsc.org.uk/genuki/REG/nry.htm
  Between 1837 and 1930

- Registration Districts in Yorkshire; West Riding
  www.fhsc.org.uk/genuki/REG/wry.htm
  Between 1837 and 1930

- [St. Catherine's House Marriage Index, Jan-March, 1849. District 22. Yorkshire]
  www.cs.ncl.ac.uk/genuki/StCathsTranscriptions/CATH4922.TXT

- [St. Catherine's House Marriage Index, Jan-March, 1849. District 23. Yorkshire]
  www.cs.ncl.ac.uk/genuki/StCathsTranscriptions/CATH4923.TXT

- Sheffield & District Family History Society: Registration Districts
  www.sheffieldfhs.org.uk/serv_con/reg.htm
  List of parishes and their registration districts in Sheffield area

- Yorkshire BMD: Births Marriages and Deaths on the Internet
  www.yorkshirebmd.org.uk/
  Index to civil registers held by district registrars

- The Tees Valley Indexes
  www.middlesbrough-indexes.co.uk/
  Details of an index to civil registers at registration offices in Middlesbrough, Hartlepool, Stockton on Tees, and Redcar & Cleveland. The index itself is not yet on-line

Parish & Non-Parochial Registers: Introductory Pages & Lists

- Colin Blanchard Withers' *Yorkshire Parish Registers*
  www.genuki.org.uk/big/eng/YKS/misc/CBW/YPRsIndex.html
  Details of parish registers on the Yorkshire Genuki site are taken from this book

- Registers of Baptisms, Marriages and Burials deposited at the Borthwick Institute, University of York
  www.york.ac.uk/inst/bihr/guideleaflets/angliparreg.pdf

- Yorkshire Parish Registers: Yorkshire Archaeological Society Parish Register Section
  www.yorkshireparishregisters.com/index.htm
  List of published parish registers for sale; also unpublished transcripts in the Society's library

- Family and Local History Alphabet
  www.doncaster.gov.uk/Leisure_in_Doncaster/Museums_and_history/Archives_and_Local_history/family_local_history/Local_and_Family_History_Links.asp
  Includes pages listing parish registers, bishops' transcripts, cemetery registers, non-parochial registers, *etc.,* held by Doncaster Archives

- East Riding Libraries Museums and Archives. Archives: the records we hold
  www.eastriding.gov.uk/libraries/archives/records.html
  Includes the following pages: 'Handlist of Parish Registers on Deposit', 'Handlist of Non-Anglican Church Records', Handlist of Society of Friends & Non-Parochial Registers on Microfiche', 'Cemetery Records', *etc.*
  www.eastriding.gov.uk/libraries/archives/records.html

- Archival Collections: Parish Records: A List
  www.hull.ac.uk/arc/collection/parish.html
  At the University of Hull; includes a few transcripts of registers

- Yorkshire
  www.sog.org.uk/prc/yorkshire.html
  Parish registers, printed, typescript, *etc.,* in the library of the Society of Genealogists

- Yorkshire Parish Registers in the Australian National Library
  www.pcug.org.au/~bthompso/natlib/yprxy.txt
  List of published registers

- Quaker Family History Society: Yorkshire
  www.rootsweb.com/~engqfhs/Research/counties/yorks.htm
  Notes on Quaker records

Marriage Licences

- Yorkshire: Paver's Marriage Licences for the Year 1567 to 1628
  www.genuki.org.uk/big/eng/YKS/Misc/Transcriptions/YKS/PaversIndex.html
  From the *Yorkshire Archaeological and Topographical Journal*

Indexes

- Boyd's Marriage Index: Parishes and Period of Records: Yorkshire
  www.britishorigins.com/help/popup-aboutbo-bmi-parish.htm
  Click on 'Yorkshire'
- North Yorkshire and County Durham Baptisms
  www.familyhistoryonline.co.uk/database/ClevelandFHSbaps.shtml
  Pay per view; mainly from the North Riding
- North Yorkshire Non-Conformist Baptisms
  www.familyhistoryonline.co.uk/database/ClevelandFHSNCbap.shtml
  Pay per view; from various Methodist circuits based on Guisborough, 19-20th c.
- National Burial Index (Cleveland F.H.S.)
  www.familyhistoryonline.co.uk/databAe/NBIClevelandFHS.shtml
  Pay per view; covers parts of North Yorkshire and southern Co. Durham
- National Burial Index (Huddersfield & District F.H.S.)
  www.familyhistoryonline.co.uk/database/NBIHuddersfieldDFHS.shtml
  Pay per view
- National Burial Index: (Yorkshire Archaeological Society F.H.Section)
  www.familyhistoryonline.co.uk/database/NBIYorksArchSoc.shtml
  Pay per view; covers the Leeds area, mainly 19th c.
- National Burial Index (Morley & District F.H.G.)
  www.familyhistoryonline.co.uk/database/NBIMorleyDFHG.shtml
  Pay per view; mainly 1813-37
- The Pontefract & District Family History Society Search Services
  freespace.virgin.net/richard.lockwood/
  Details of parish register databases, *etc.*
- Pontefract District Baptisms
  www.familyhistoryonline.co.uk/database/PontefractDFHSbaps.shtml
  Pay per view index to registers for 19 parishes
- Pontefract.Marriages
  www.familyhistoryonline.co.uk/database/PontefractDFHSmar.shtml
  Pay per view index to 21 parish registers in the area
- Pontefract District Burials
  www.familyhistoryonline.co.uk/database/PontefractDFHSbur.shtml
  Pay per view index to parish registers for Ackworth, Featherstone, Pontefract, Normanton, *etc.*
- National Burial Index (Rotherham Family History Society)
  www.familyhistoryonline.co.uk/database/NBIRotherhamFHS.shtml
  Pay per view; mainly 19th c.
- National Burial Index (Sheffield and District Family History Society)
  www.familyhistoryonline.co.uk/database/NBISheffieldDFHS.shtml
  Pay per view; includes parishes around Sheffield, including Dore and Norton in Derbyshire
- Wakefield District Marriages (1813-1837)
  www.familyhistoryonline.co.uk/database/WakefieldDFHSMarr.shtml
  Pay per view index to 23 parish registers in the area
- National Burial Index (City of York and District Family History Society)
  www.familyhistoryonline.co.uk/database/NBCityofYorkDFHS.shtml
  Pay per view
- IGI Batch Numbers for Yorkshire, England
  freepages.genealogy.rootsweb.com/-hughwallis/IGIBatchNumbers/CountyYorkshire_(A-D).HTM
  Continued on 5 further pages
- Yorkshire, England, parish and probate records
  www.ancestry.co.uk/search/db.aspx?dbid=5982
  Click on title. Index to published registers, *etc.*
- Quaker Archives Database/Leeds University Library
  www.leeds.ac.uk/library/spcoll/quaker/quakint1.htm
  Includes indexes to some Yorkshire Quaker births, marriages and deaths

- Yorkshire Quaker Heritage Project
  www.learndev.hull.ac.uk/quaker/
  Includes information on Quaker 'digests', i.e. registers

- Isle of Axholme Yorkshire Strays
  www.genuki.org.uk/big/eng/YKS/Misc/IOAStrays.html
  Index of Methodist baptisms

- Hearts of Oak
  www.geocities.com/Heartland/Ridge/8482/HeartsOfOak/coverpage.html
  Includes a number of Roman Catholic Registers

Newspapers

- Death Notices in Yorkshire Newspapers
  homepage.ntl.world.com/jeffery.knaggs/YD.html
  17,000 entries, mostly for 1901

Publications

- Publications Available from the Cleveland, North Yorkshire and South Durham Family History Society
  www.clevelandfhs.org.uk/Publications.htm
  Includes parish register transcriptions for the Cleveland area of Co. Durham and Yorkshire

- [Doncaster Family History Society Publications]
  www.doncasterfhs.co.uk/
  Click on 'Publications'. Includes cemetery burial register, marriage indexes, burial indexes, *etc.*

- Huddersfield & District Family History Society Publications
  www.hdfhs.org.uk/fhspubtp.htm
  Includes parish registers

- The Pontefract and District Family History Society: Publications
  freespace.virgin.net/richard.lockwood/publications.htm
  Includes baptism, marriage and burial transcripts and indexes, *etc.*

- Rotherham Family History Society Publications
  www.rotherhamfhs.co.uk
  Includes a few registers

- Sheffield & District Family History Society: Society Publications: Microfiche
  www.sheffieldfhs.org.uk/Pub_con/publications.html
  Includes register transcripts and indexes

- Wakefield & District Family History Society: Society Publications
  www.wdfhs.co.uk/publications.html
  Includes marriage and burial indexes, parish registers, *etc.*

- Wharfedale Family History Group Parish Registers
  web.onetel.net.uk/~gdlawson/wfhg/pubs1.htm

- The City of York & District Family History Society: Society Publications
  www.yorkfamilyhistory.org.uk/publications.htm
  Includes parish registers and indexes, *etc.*

- Brian Jones
  www.brianjoneswry.com
  Includes various transcripts of West Riding parish registers for sale

Ackworth

- Ackworth St. Cuthbert, Yorkshire: Parish Register Transcriptions
  freepages.genealogy.rootsweb.com/~petyt/ackprt.htm
  Baptisms 1813-40; banns 1823-53

Batley Carr

- Batley Carr: Transcription of the Baptisms 1841-1862
  www.genuki.org.uk/big/eng/YKS/Misc/Transcriptions/WRY/BatleyCarrBaptisms.html
  Continued to 1866 at **/BatleyCarrBaptisms1863_1866.html**

Bolsterstone

- Bolsterstone Genealogy Project
  www.bolsterstone.de/
  Index to baptisms 1778-1872, & marriages 1868-1905

- Bolsterstone: Transcription of the Bolsterstone Christenings 1778 to 1813 in date order
  www.genuki.org.uk/big/eng/YKS/Misc/Transcriptions/WRY/BolsterstoneBaptisms1778-1813.html
  For 'in date order', see: **/BolsterstoneBaptisms1778-1813d.html**

- Bolsterstone: Transcription of Bolsterstone Marriages 1868-1877
  www.genuki.org.uk/big/eng/YKS/Misc/Transcriptions/WRY/BolsterstoneMarriages1868-77.html

Bradford

- Bradford Parish Church Burials
  www.familyhistoryonline.co.uk/database/BradfordFHSBurials.shtml
  Pay per view; covers 1681-1837
- Name Index to Bradford Church Burials 1681-1837
  www.genuki.org.uk/big/eng/YKS/bfhs/pcbur81.html
  Details of published indexes for sale

Brawby
See Salton

Burghwallis

- Burghwallis Roman Catholic Church Baptisms
  www.doncasterfhs.fhs.co.uk/members/burghw.htm
  Downloadable files for 1761-1782 and 1798-1836

Burmantofts

- Beckett Street Cemetery
  www.fobsc.20m.com/
  Also known as Burmantofts Cemetery, Leeds. Introduction; includes fiche for sale of the burial and grave registers and inscriptions

Burneston

- Burneston: Burneston Parish Registers, Baptisms, some years, 1738-1805
  www.genuki.org.uk/big/eng/YKS/Misc/Transcriptions/NRY/BurnestonBaptisms1738-1805.html
  For 1784-5, see **/BurnestonBaptisms1784-5.html**
- Burneston: Burneston Parish Registers 1738-9
  www.genuki.org.uk/big/eng/YKS/Misc/Transcriptions/NRY/BurnestonPRs1738-9.html
  Baptisms and marriages. For 1754-5, see **/BurnestonPRs1754-5.html**
- Burneston: Burneston Parish Registers, Marriages: 1741-3, 1751-3
  www.genuki.org.uk/big/eng/Yks/Misc/Transcriptions/NRY/BurnestonMarriages1741-53.html
  For 1788-1782, see **/BurnestonMarriages1780-2.html**
- Burneston: Burneston Parish Registers, Burials, some years 1740-1782
  www.genuki.org.uk/big/eng/YKS/Misc/Transcriptions/NRY/BurnestonBurials1740-1782.html
  Continued as follows:
  1788-1806 **/BurnestonBurials.html**
  1828 **/BurnestonBurials1828.html**

Calverley
See also Idle

- Calverley Parish Baptisms Index 1574-1644
  www.genuki.org.uk/big/eng/YKS/Misc/Transcriptions/WRY/CalverleyBaptismsIndex1574-1644.html
- Calverley: All legible Baptisms and Births recorded at the Parish Church of Calverley for Families in the Idle / Thackley / Windhill area 1726 to 1745
  www.genuki.org.uk/big/eng/YKS/Misc/Transcriptions/WRY/Calverley__IdleBaptisms1726-45.html
- Calverley Parish Marriage Index 1596-1720
  www.genuki.org.uk/big/eng/YKS/Misc/Transcriptions/WRY/CalverleyMarriagesIndex1596-1720.html
- Parish Church of Calverley: Marriages 1813 to 1834: sorted alphabetically by Groom
  www.genuki.org.uk/big/eng/YKS/MISC/Transcriptions/WRY/CalverleyMarriagesGrooms1813-34.html
  For brides, see **/CalverleyMarriages1813-34.html**
  Continued to 1843 at **/CalverleyMarriagesG1837-43.html** and **/CalverleyMarriagesB1837-43.html**
- Calverley
  www.calverley.info/
  Enter, click on title & on 'Calverley'. Includes baptisms 1574-1840, banns 1772-6, marriages 1596-1930, & burials 1596-1860

- Calverley Parish Burials Index 1596-1720
  www.genuki.org.uk/big/eng/YKS/Misc/Transcriptions/WRY/ClverleyBurialsIndex1596-1720.html

Cayton

- Cayton: Transcription of Baptisms from the Film of the Bishops' Transcripts
  www.genuki.org.uk/big/eng/YKS/Misc/Transcriptions/NRY/CaytonBaptisms1812to1860.html
  Covers 1812-37 and 1860
- Cayton: Transcription of Marriages from the Film of the Bishops' Transcripts
  www.genuki.org.uk/big/eng/YKS/Misc/NRY/CaytonMarriages1812to1860.html
  Covers 1812-37
- Cayton: Transcription of Burials from the Film of the Bishops' Transcripts
  www.genuki.org.uk/big/eng/YKS/Misc/Transcriptions/NRY/CaytonBurials1812to1860.html

Cowesby

- North Yorkshire and County Durham Marriages
  www.familyhistoryonline.co.uk/database/ClevelandFHSmar.shtml
  Pay per view index for Cowesby, Middleton on Leven, Stokesley and Welbury parish registers/bishops' transcripts

Dewsbury

- Dewsbury: Transcription of the Dewsbury Baptisms 1841 to 1866
  www.genuki.org.uk/big/eng/YKS/Misc/Transcriptions/WRY/DewsburyBaptisms1841-66.html
- Dewsbury Transcription of the Burials 1813 to 1817
  www.genuki.org.uk/big/eng/YKS/Misc/Transcriptions/WRY/DewsburyBurials1813to1817.html
  Continued as follows:
  1818-1822 **/DewsburyBurials1818to1822.html**
  1885-1886 **/DewsburyBurials1885-86.html**

Doncaster

- St. George's Burials 1578-1855
  www.doncasterfhs.freeserve.co.uk/members/
  Click on title. Downloadable file for Doncaster Family History Society members only

Eccleshill

- Bradford Burial Index
  www.familyhistoryonline.co.uk/database/BradfordFHSbur.shtml
  Pay per view index to registers from Eccleshill parish church, 1842-1994, and Norman Lane Wesleyan Burial Ground, Eccleshill
- Norman Lane Burial Ground, Eccleshill, Bradford (1823-1984)
  www.genuki.org.uk/big/eng/YKS/bfhs/nlbg.html
  Details of published registers *etc.,* for sale

Egton

- Earliest post-Recusant Register: Egton
  www.geocities.com/Heartland/Ridge/8482/HeartsOfOak/returns5.html
  Baptisms & marriages, early 19th c.

Elland

- Elland St. Mary's Baptism Registers (1559-1850)
  www.familyhistoryonline.co.uk/database/CFHSEllandStMarysBap.shtml
  Pay per view; covers 1646-1850
- Elland St. Mary's Marriage Registers (1649-1837)
  www.familyhistoryonline.co.uk/database/CFHSEllandStMarysMarr.shtml
  Pay per view
- Elland St. Mary's Burial Registers (1714-1843)
  www.familyhistoryonline.co.uk/database/CFHSEEllandStMaryBur.shtml
  Pay per view index
- Elland Parish Church: Marriages 1754 to 1812
  www.whitwam.freeserve.co.uk/ell.htm
  Details of indexes for sale

Farsley

- Farsley St. John's Parish Church Records
  www.calverley.info/fars_par_rec.htm
  Includes marriages, 1845-1950

Forcett

- Forcett: Transcription of the Baptisms 1596 to 1649
  www.genuki.org.uk/big/eng/YKS/Misc/Transcriptions/NRY/ForcettBaptisms1596_1707.html

  Continued as follows:
  1813-1857 **/ForcettBaptisms1813-1857.html**
  1857-1861 **/ForcettBaptisms1857_1861.html**

- Forcett: Transcription of the Forcett Marriages 1606-1812
  www.genuki.org.uk/big/eng/YKS/Misc/Transcriptions/NRY/ForcettMarriages1597_1812.html

- Forcett: Transcription of the Burials 1813-1898
  www.genuki.org.uk/big/eng/YKS/Misc/Transcriptions/NRY/ForcettBurials1813_1898.html

Guisborough

See also Redcar & Skelton

- Guisborough Primitve Methodist Circuit Register of Baptisms 1850-1903
  www.clevelandfhs.org.uk/guis_prim_meth.htm

- Guisborough Wesleyan Methodist Circuit Register of Baptisms 1840-1914
  www.clevelandfhs.org.uk/wesleyan_guis_.htm

Halifax

- Halifax Parish Church Registers 1542-5
  www.genuki.org.uk/big/eng/YKS/WRY/Halifax/Halifax1542.html
  Transcribed from *Yorkshire County Magazine*

- Halifax St. John's Baptism Registers
  www.familyhistoryonline.co.uk/database/CFHSHalifaxStJohnsBap.shtml
  Pay per view. Covers 1813-38

- Halifax St. John's Marriage Registers
  www.familyhistoryonline.co.uk/database/CFHSHalifaxStJohnsMarr.shtml

  Pay per view; covers 1754-1837

- Halifax St. John's Burial Registers
  www.familyhistoryonline.co.uk/database/CFHSHalifaxStJohnsBur.shtml

  Pay per view index, 1813-1937

Hartshead

- Hartshead: Transcription of the St. Peter's, Hartshead Burials, 1692 to 1722
  www.genuki.org.uk/big/eng/YKS/Misc/Transcriptions/WRY/HartsheadStPeterBur1692-1733.html

  Continued as follows:
  1733-1785 **/HartsheadStPeterBur1733-1785.html**
  1786-1812 **/HartsheadStPeterBur1786-1812.html**

- Hartshead Burials 1890-93
  freepages.genealogy.rootsweb.com/~hartsheadcumclifton/hartshead/bur.htm

Hatfield

- Hatfield Parish Register Extracts
  freepages.genealogy.rootsweb.com/~maureenbryson/id52.htm
  Extracts only, 1572-1832

Hawnby

- Hawnby Bishops' Transcripts: Births and Christenings 1723 to 1852
  www.genuki.org.uk/big/eng/YKS/Misc/Transcriptions/NRY/HawnbyBTsIndex.html

- Hawnby Bishops' Transcripts: Marriages
  www.genuki.org.uk/big/eng/YKS/Misc/Transcriptions/NRY/HawnbyMarriages1.html

High Bentham

- Low Bentham parish: High Bentham Burials Transcription
  www.genuki.org.uk/big/eng/YKS/WRY/Lowbentham/BrHighBenthamBurials.html

  Covers 1944-2000

Honley

- Honley Cemetery Burial Book
  www.honley.ukf.net/burialbook.htm
  Covers 1850-1930

Horbury

- Horbury: Transcription of Horbury Baptisms and Burials 1770 to 1791
  www.genuki.org.uk/big/eng/YKS/Misc/Transcriptions/WRY/HorburyBapBur1770-1791.html
  Continued to 1812 on 3 further pages
- Horbury Marriages 1774 to 1812
  www.genuki.org.uk/big/eng/YKS/Misc/Transcriptions/WRY/HorburyMar1774-1812.html

Huddersfield

- Huddersfield Parish Church Marriages 1754 to 1837
  www.whitwam.freeserve.co.uk/hpcm2.htm
  Details of indexes for sale

Hunslet

- National Burial Index: Leeds, Hunslet Cemetery
  www.familyhistoryonline.co.uk/database/NBI_HUNS.shtml
  Pay per view

Idle

- Idle Parish Church Records
  www.calverley.info/idle_par_rec.htm
  Includes index of baptisms to 1829, & burials 1831-9
- Calverley Parish Registers, Idle Chapel Baptisms 1796 to 1800
  www.genuki.org.uk/big/eng/YKS/Misc/Transcriptions/WRY/IdleChapelBaptisms1796-1800.html

Kilnwick on the Wolds

- All Saints Church Parish Registers, Kilnwick on the Wolds, ERY
  freepages.genealogy.rootsweb.com/~pbtyc/Den/Kilnwick/Index.html
  Baptisms 1813-41; banns 1823-41; marriages 1813-36; burials 1823-41
- Kilnwick on the Wolds: Transcript from All Saints Parish Register, Kilnwick on the Wolds ERY: Baptisms 1813-1828
  www.genuki.org.uk/big/eng/YKS/Misc/Transcriptions/ERY/KilnwickBaptisms1813-1828.html
  Continued to 1841 at **/KilnwickBaptisms1829-1841.html**
  Indexed at **/KilnwickBaptismsChildIndex1813-1841.html**
- Kilnwick on the Wolds: Transcription of the Kilnwick on the Wolds Parish Register: Banns 1823-1841
  www.genuki.org.uk/big/eng/YKS/Misc/Transcriptions/ERY/KilnwickBanns1823-1841.html
  Indexed at **/KilnwickBannsIndex1823-41.html**
- Kilnwick on the Wolds: Transcript from All Saints Parish Register, Kilnwick on the Wolds, ERY: Marriages 1813-1841
  www.genuki.org.uk/big/eng/YKS/Misc/Transcriptions/ERY/KilnwickMarriages1813-1841.html
  Indexed at **/KilnwickMarriagesIndex1813-1841.html**
- Kilnwick on the Wolds: Transcript from All Saints Parish Register, Kilnwick on the Wolds ERY: Burials 1813-1841
  www.genuki.org.uk/big/eng/YKS/Misc/Transcriptions/ERY/KilnwickBurials1813-1841.html
  Indexed at **/KilnwickBurialsIndex1813-1841.html**

Kirklington

- Kirklington: The Kirklington Parish Registers, part of 1803 to 1812: Marriages
  www.genuki.org.uk/big/eng/YKS/Misc/Transcriptions/NRY/KirklingtonPRs1803-12.htm

Leeds

- Churches, Chapels & Cemeteries
  leedsindexers.co.uk/Main-Churches.htm
  List for Leeds
- Leeds Parish Registers 1612-1639
  www.bigenealogy.com/leeds/
  As published by the Thoresby Society
- Leeds: Transcription of the St. Paul's, Leeds, Burials 1796 to 1819
  www.genuki.org.uk/big/eng/YKS/Misc/Transcriptions/WRY/LeedsStPaulBur1796-1819.html

- Leeds General Cemetery Company Ltd.
  www.leeds.ac.uk/spcoll/handlists/O4OMS421_woodhouse.pdf
  Calendar of records held in the Brotherton Library, University of Leeds, including burial registers

Malton

- Transcriptions of the Births Marriages and Deaths from the *Malton Messenger* for the year 1854
  www.genuki.org.uk/big/eng/YKS/Misc/Transcriptions/NRY/MaltonMessenger1854BDM.html
  Further annual pages cover the period to 1865
- Births Marriages & Deaths from the *Malton Messenger* 1854
  www.angelfire.com/de/BobSanders/Malton54.html
  Continued to 1860 on 10 further pages

Middleton on Leven
See Cowesby

Morley

- Morley District Baptisms and Marriages
  www.familyhistoryonline.co.uk/database/WRYMorley.shtml
  Pay per view index mainly from Morley, Rothwell and Woodkirk 18-20th c.

Normanby

- Transcript of St. Andrews Parish Church, Normanby, NRY, Parish Registers
  freepages.genealogy.rootsweb.com/~pbtyc/Den/Normanby/index.html
  Baptisms 1699-1812; marriages 1699-1837; burials 1700-1812
- Normanby: Transcription of the Parish Registers: Baptisms 1699-1774
  www.genuki.org.uk/big/eng/YKS/Misc/Transcriptions/NRY/NormanbyBaptisms1699.html
  Continued to 1812 at **/Normanby Baptisms 1775.html**
  Indexed at **/NormanbyBaptismsIndex.html**
- Normanby: Transcription of the Normanby Parish Registers: Marriages 1699-1750
  www.genuki.org.uk/big/eng/YKS/Misc/Transcriptions/NRY/NormanbyMarriages1699-1750.html
  Continued to 1837 (including index) on 3 further pages
- Normanby: Transcription of the Normanby Parish Registers: Burials 1700-1812
  www.genuki.org.uk/big/eng/YKS/Misc/Transcriptions/NRY/NormanbyBurials1700-1812.html
  Indexed at **/NormanbyBurialsIndex.html**
- Normanby Parish Registers: Burials: Notes
  www.genuki.org.uk/big/eng/YKS/Misc/Transcriptions/NRY/ormanbyPRNotes.html

Northowram

- Nonconformist Register of Baptisms, Marriages and Deaths ... 1644-1702, 1702-1752, generally known as the Northowram or Coley Register, but comprehending numerous notices of puritans and anti-puritans in Yorkshire, Lancashire, Cheshire, London, &c.
  www.genuki.org.uk/big/eng/YKS/northowram/
  From a printed book published 1881

Pudsey

- Pudsey Parish Church Records
  www.calverley.info/pud_par_rec.htm
  Includes baptisms 1661-1845, & marriages 1838-1900

Rawmarsh
See Wath upon Dearne

Redcar

- Guisborough Wesleyan Methodist Circuit Register of Baptisms: Redcar Section, 1860-1926
  www.clevelandfhs.org.uk/wesleyan_redcar.htm

Roos

- Roos Parish Registers
  www.pcug.org.au/~bthompso/roos/readme.htm
  Scanned transcript of a register originally published 1888, covering 1571-1679.

Rosedale

- Rosedale People: an index
  www.genuki.org.uk/big/eng/YKS/Misc/Transcriptions/NRYRosedale/
  Sources indexed include parish registers

Rotherham

- Rotherham Parish Register Extracts
  freepages.genealogy.rootsweb.com/~maureenbryson/id51.htm
  Extracts only, 1542-1784

Rothwell

See Morley

Salton

- Transcription from St. John's Parish Register, Salton and Brawby, Vale of Pickering, NRY, for the period 1573-1837
  freepages.genealogy.rootsweb.com/~pbtyc/Den/Salton_and_Brawby/Index.html
  Baptisms & marriages, 1573-1837

- Salton: Transcript from St. John's Parish Register, Salton and Brawby, Vale of Pickering, NRY: Baptisms 1573-1600
  www.genuki.org.uk/big/eng/YKS/Misc/Transcriptions/NRY/SaltonBaptisms1573-1600.html
  Continued to 1837 on 5 further pages, plus 3 pages of indexes

- Salton: Transcript from St. John's Parish Register, Salton and Brawby, Vale of Pickering, NRY: Marriages 1573-1650
  www.genuki.org.uk/big/eng/YKS/Misc/Transcriptions/NRY/SaltonMarriages1573-1650.html
  Continued to 1837 on 5 further pages, plus indexes to brides, grooms and witnesses

Sandtoft

- Sandtoft
  privatewww.essex.ac.uk/~alan/family/G-Sandtoft.html
  Extracts from a Huguenot register, 17th c.

Sheffield

- Sheffield & District BDM Registers: Timelines
  www.sheffieldfhs.org.uk/data/registers.html
  List of registers and dates

- Sheffield & District Family History Society: Transcription Projects
  www.sheffieldfhs.org.uk/serv_con/transcrips.html
  Details of the society's Burials transcriptions project, *etc.*

- Sheffield Parish Register Extracts
  freepages.genealogy.rootsweb.com/~maureenbryson/id50.htm
  Extracts only, 1565-1853

Skelton

- Guisborough Wesleyan Methodist Circuit Register of Baptisms, Skelton Section 1869-1926
  www.clevelandfhs.org.uk/wesleyan_skelton.htm

South Milford

- South Milford: Trnascription of the Burials 1847 to 1979
  www.genuki.org.uk/big/eng/YKS/Misc/transcriptions/WRY/SouthMilfordBurials1847_1979.html
  Continued to 1998 at **/SouthMilfordBurials1979_1998.html**

Staincross

- Burial Register for St. John the Evangelist Church, Staincross
  freepages.genealogy.rootsweb.com/~framland/stcr/stjscd1.htm
  Index

Stanningley

- Stanningley St. Thomas Parish Church Records
  www.calverley.info/stan_par_rec.htm
  Includes marriages, 1863-1950

Stokesley

See Cowesby

Thorne

- Thorne Parish Register Extracts
  freepages.genealogy.rootsweb.com/~maureenbryson/id53.htm
  Extracts, 1619-1888

Ugthorpe

- Earliest post-Recusant Registers: Ugthorpe
  www.geocities.com/Heartland/Ridge/8482/HeartsOfOak/returns4.html
  Baptism & marriage registers, 1788-1840, *etc.*

Wakefield

- Burials in the Parish Church
  freepages.genealogy.rootsweb.com/~framland/CHURCH/burials.htm
  At Wakefield

Wath upon Dearne

- Wath & Dearne Valley Resources Site
  www.gleaden.plus.com/index.htm
  Click on 'parish registers'. Includes Wath baptisms 1598-1778; marriages 1598-1779; burials 1598-1778; also, for Rawmarsh, baptisms 1653-1672; marriages 1575-1753; burials 1558-1633

Welbury

See Cowesby

West Witton

- West Witton: Transcription of the Burials 1822-1846
  www.genuki.org.uk/big/eng/YKS/Misc/Transcriptions/NRY/WestWittonBurials.html

Wetherby

- Wetherby: Transcription of the Wetherby Burials 1848 to 1866, 1869, & 1871 (Jan and Feb)
  www.genuki.org.uk/big/eng/YKS/Misc/Transcriptions/WRY/WetherbyBurials1848-71.html

Whitby

- A Complete Transcript of the Whitby 'Non-Parochial' Registers at the P.R.O., London RG/4/3707; Roman Catholic baptisms 1794-1840, marriages 1806-1835, & deaths 1818-25
  www.geocities.com/Heartland/Ridge/8482/HeartsOfOak/returns6.html

- Marriages Transcribed from 1828 Copy of the *Whitby Repository & Monthly Miscellany*
  www.clevelandfhs.org.uk/whitby%201828.htm

Whitkirk

- Whitkirk: Transcription of the Burials 1875-1879
  www.genuki.org.uk/big/eng/YKS/Misc/Transcriptions/WRY/WhitkirkBurials1875to9.html

Woodkirk

See Morley

Worsbrough

- Swaithe Main Colliery Disaster, Worsbrough
  www.barnsleyfhs.co.uk/swaithe1.htm
  List of miners killed, 1875

York

- The Register of Burials in York Minster, accompanied by Monumental Inscriptions, and illustrated with biographied notices
  www.genuki.org.uk/big/eng/YKS/Misc/MIs/ARY/YorkMinsterBurialsindex.html
  Covers 1634-1836; originally published in the *Yorkshire archaeological and topographical journal,* vol.1, 1870.

- The Register of Marriages in York Minster, illustrated with biographical notices, 1681 to 1762
  www.genuki.org.uk/big/eng/YKS/Misc/Transcriptions/ARY/YorkMinsterMarriagesIndex.html
  Originally published in the *Yorkshire Archaeological & Topographical journal,* vol. 1, 1870

- York Cemetery
  homepages.tesco.net/~hugh.murray/home.htm
  Database of c.123,000 burial records since 1837